A. J. LAND, CHIEF

MAYOR
J. W. ROMAINE
CITY COUNCIL
CHAS. F. NOLTE
S. B. VANZANDT
GEO. C. BLAKESLEE
GEO. BUTLER
S. E. MULLIN
E. M. ADAMS
EDW. J. OLEARY

OFFICE OF
CHIEF

Bellingham Fire Department

Bellingham, Wash., MAY 18 1905 *1905*

Manager
Pacific American Fisheries Co
Bennet Ave foot of Harris
City.

Dear Sir:

There is now in preparation a Historical Souvenir of the Bellingham Fire Department, which will be finely illustrated with copper-plate engravings of everyone connected with the Department, the fire houses, apparatus, etc. The proceeds will be turned into the Relief Fund for the benefit of any member of the Department who may be disabled or meet with accidental death while in the performance of his duties.

We, the members of the Bellingham Fire Department, desire to make this publication a financial success, and to that end we solicit your hearty co-operation. A representative will call upon you shortly and explain the work, and any assistance you may favor us with will be greatly appreciated by

Very respectfully yours,

BELLINGHAM FIRE DEPARTMENT,

A. J. Land Chief.

Ninety-nine years ago, Fire A.J. Chief Land solicited support for "a Historical Souvenir", the printed history of the area's fire service.

Bellingham Fire Department

The First 100 Years

FOREWORD

The colorful history of the Bellingham Fire Department (BFD) mirrors the growth and change in the community it serves: one hundred years of expanding boundaries, population growth, technical advances, changes in the law, and increasing demand for more services, more sophistication.

From the volunteer brigades and their leather buckets of the 1890s, to the computers and radios in use today, from two fire stations in 1904 to the present necklace of six stations that encircles the City, BFD has changed radically, responding to the social evolution that is our local history. In the beginning, fire suppression was the only concern. But today's BFD is also the lead local agency for emergency medical services, hazardous chemical spills, technical rescue, and the modern phenomenon of terrorism.

A group within the current fire department regards the advent of BFD's centennial as a solemn responsibility. BFD's one-hundredth birthday happens "on our watch," and the task of documenting that history is both a duty and an honor.

Compiling the stories and images seen here would have been impossible without the dedicated foresight of local historian Galen Biery. We are also indebted to retired Herald photographer Jack Carver and his watchful eye. Both men made generous gifts of their images to the archives of the community's museum so that we, and future generations, can look back more clearly on our past.

Special appreciation goes to Jeff Jewell and Toni Nagel at the Whatcom Museum of History and Art for their enthusiastic support and cooperation. Local 106 of the International Association of Fire Fighters provided the financial foundation for our risky venture. The Center for Pacific Northwest Studies made valuable contributions, and many retirees made their personal keepsakes available.

To birth and nurture this snapshot of BFD's history, dozens of dispatchers, paramedics, firefighters, and administrative staff volunteered their time, their skills, and their energy. The enormous responsibility of coordinating these resources belonged to two people: Captain Mike Larson, who had both the original vision and the tireless commitment to follow it, and Facilities Development Manager Dave Wolf, whose enthusiasm and attention to detail elevated the quality of this book immeasurably. Firefighter Michael B. Wallace was a constant contributor and source of inspiration. Other sub-committee chairs and significant contributors were Chris Behee, Brian Cain, Jay Comfort, Sean Farnand, Ryan Gilbert, Kurt Jensen, Jason Sims, Greg Sluys, and Jerry Stougard. We are not journalists, historians, or graphic artists, and in the end it was the unselfish support of others that helped us achieve something beyond our original dream.

Everyone involved hopes each reader will find within these pages the color and intrigue that has been the continuing story of BFD for the first one hundred years.

 • ISBN: 1-932129-75-8

Published by Pediment Publishing, a division of The Pediment Group, Inc. www.pediment.com

Table of Contents

1996.10.2398 Biery Collection-Whatcom Museum

The stern expressions and contrived pose imply that this meeting, held at the doors to a local saloon in the summer heat of 1890, had a purpose. Conrad Mayer, on the left, was Chief of the New Whatcom fire brigades, and evidently used his wardrobe to make sure everyone knew it. On the right is A.J. Gibson, foreman for the Bennett Hose Company No. 1, in Fairhaven. The "SFD" on Mayer's belt buckle is a remnant from the old Sehome Fire Department. Sehome changed its name to New Whatcom April 18, 1890.

THE BRIGADES ERA

Before There Was A BFD...

By Captain Mike Larson

From the settlement of Bellingham Bay in 1852 until 1889, the only fire protection in the struggling communities of Whatcom, Sehome, Bellingham and Fairhaven was frantic bystanders in bucket brigades. On August 7, 1889, Pioneer Hook and Ladder Company No.1 was founded, with the motto "Ready for Duty." Soon fire companies were organized in all of Bellingham Bay's small cities, a measure of the enthusiasm and vigor with which these towns were growing. By December 1893 there were a total of three hook and ladder and six hose companies complete with response districts, alliances, and rivalries.

The men of these early fire companies were greatly admired. It was quite a feather in one's cap, both socially and politically, to be associated with such a group. Often prominent businessmen, or other community leaders, would strive to be foreman (chief) or 1st assistant foreman (assistant chief) of a company to enhance their prestige.

The men in the brigades took great pride in out-doing their rival fire laddies, not just in beating the competition to a fire or during a competitive fire company muster, but also putting on a flashier show during a community parade or hosting a better fireman's ball.

In the beginning, the fire brigades' equipment was basic at best. Initially they used hand-pulled hose carts mounted with hose reels holding over 500 feet of canvas or rubber 2.5" hose. Hook and ladder companies pulled heavy wagons laden with ladders and pike poles of various lengths. Up to a dozen firefighters sweated and toiled to pull their equipment up the many steep hills surrounding Bellingham Bay, and struggled to control that equipment going down. Most of the streets were dirt, or even thigh deep with mud. These brave laddies were only paid when actually working at fires. Sometimes those wages would not even cover the cost of trousers that were burnt or torn.

Up until the construction of a fire hall at 209 E. Chestnut Street in 1890, Pioneer Hook and Ladder Co. held their meetings in Daniel McKinnon and Conrad Mayer's blacksmith shop. The new station was wood frame, with corrugated metal siding and roofing and a large bell tower that served as fire alarm and meeting announcer.

In March 1890, some Pioneer members acquired their own hose cart and broke away to form Sehome Hose Co. No. 1. The remaining Pioneer firefighters changed their name to Bellingham Hook and Ladder Co. No. 1, but then changed the name back eleven days later. In 1891, Pioneer and Sehome dismantled their fire hall and relocated to 1113 N. Forest St. This would be home to both companies until they disbanded in 1904 at the creation of the unified City of Bellingham Fire Department.

Sehome Hose Co. No. 1's first foreman was John Kastner. In the late 1930s, Kastner claimed that when he came to Sehome, water was selling for 25 cents a barrel, so nobody could afford a fire. "But things were soon remedied," he noted, when Bellingham Bay Improvement Co. installed a water works. "Pretty soon lots of people began having fires." One of Kastner's favorite stories was of a flue fire at the Byron Hotel. Kastner ordered that two hoses be directed down the chimney. The deluge extinguished the fire but flushed the Byron's entire stock of fine china out the front door onto Dock St. (now Cornwall Ave).

A congratulatory poster from January 25, 1892, described the gallant Sehome firemen: "The Company has responded to 25 alarms of fire since its organization. It has one hose cart and 900 feet of hose under its entire care and supervision. It has 18 active members, of whom none are laggards, but are ever ready and watching to protect our glorious city from the destructive demon, Fire."

"Deeds, not Words" was Sehome's motto. The company had won several prizes in Fourth of July parades and other hose contests of various kinds. The trophy the company prized most was a pretty silver command trumpet they won during a public voting contest, which selected Sehome Hose Company the most popular company of the fire department. Sehome Hose Company was always found at their posts of duty and lead the way where fire was raging and smoke the thickest, their word of command was "Come Boys, Not Go."

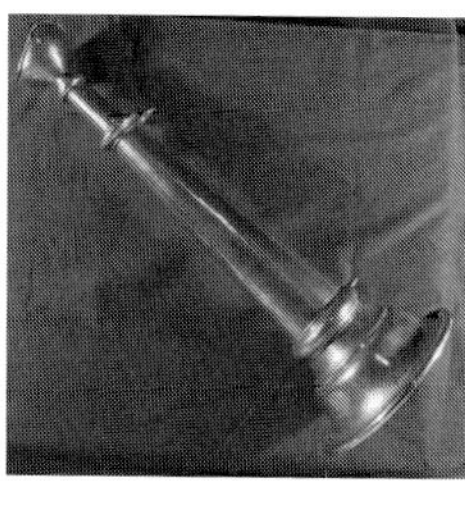

Sehome Hose Co.'s reputation was not without blemish, however. They were one of the crews, along with a Whatcom hose company, that was involved in the infamous waterfight in 1891 that doused dignitaries aboard the first Canadian Pacific Railway train to arrive in New Whatcom. The full story can be found later in this book.

Cosgrove Hose Co. No. 2, serving the community of Sehome, was organized March 26, 1890 in honor of Edmund Cosgrove. He was the mayor of New Whatcom and the financial sponsor of the company. Cosgrove Co. had 20 members, the maximum number provided by ordinance. Their original fire hall at 1221 Dock St. is remembered for its lofty cedar-shingled bell tower at the rear of the building.

In December 1899, the company relocated to the old Reveille Newspaper building at 1315 Bay St. Cosgrove would reside there until the end of the brigade era in 1904. From this central location, the company is said to have responded to more calls than any other in the area – more than 150 runs in its 14 year existence. Cosgrove's watchword was; "We Race to Save".

Whatcom Hose Company No.1, protecting the community west of Whatcom Creek, was organized March 11, 1890. Whatcom No.1 answered alarms from their quarters in the old Whatcom city hall building until the construction in April 1890 of their new quarters at 907-13th. The new fire hall was a large and commodious building with two large doorways leading into a spacious apparatus bay on the first floor. The second floor was used as a reading and meeting room. The building was surmounted with a neat sixty-foot bell tower with the inside of the tower fitted to hang and dry fire hose. Little time would pass before Whatcom Hose Co. No.1 would be sharing their new fire hall with the newly formed Whatcom Hose Co. No.2 that organized July 11, 1890. These two companies would occupy this fire station even through the first year of BFD's existence while a new fire station at 201 Prospect Street was completed in 1905 for BFD's new Combination #1 wagon.

Whatcom Hook and Ladder Co. No.2 was organized December 5, 1893 and equipped with a village ladder truck – a hand-drawn wagon with one 35' extension ladder, one 18' and one 16' single ladder and two roof ladders. Whatcom Hook and Ladder would also occupy the fire station at 907-13th Street until their disbanding in 1905.

After the amalgamation of the towns of Whatcom and Sehome in 1891, all of their four hose companies changed their names to Whatcom Nos. 1-4, but their rivalries were unchanged. Sehome's companies, Whatcom No. 1 & 2 from the east of Whatcom Creek, reveled in the chance to charge across town trying to arrive at the scene before their old competitors, now Whatcom No. 3 & 4. Once at a fire, all worked together well to suppress the fire and preserve personal property, at which they excelled.

The Fairhaven Fire Department in 1891 consisted of two hose companies and one hook and ladder company. The first of these was Bennett Hose Co. No.1, organized June 6,1890. Named in honor of Nelson Bennett, land developer, friend and staunch supporter of the City of Fairhaven. On September 2, 1891 Bennett presented to the City of Fairhaven a Silsby steam fire engine, the first of its kind in the entire Bellingham Bay area. Bennett Co. may have been quartered at 1206 Mill Street.

The other hose company in Fairhaven, also organized June 6, 1890, was Wardner Hose Co. No.2, named in honor of its sponsor and local wealthy businessman, James F. Wardner. Wardner was noted principally for the great number of successful social affairs held under its auspices, and for the unusual musical talent displayed by its members. Wardner's fine brass band was a regular feature of parades and other occasions.

Fairhaven Hook and Ladder Co. No.1 was assembled September 7, 1891. They had possession of a Preston ladder wagon. Both Fairhaven Hook and Ladder and Wardner Hose Co. responded from a hall at 1112 Donovan Street. This structure would serve as BFD Station 2 until 1927.

The volunteer brigade era would close with the disbanding of all the companies in 1904 upon the consolidation of Whatcom and Fairhaven, forming the new city of Bellingham and the Bellingham Fire Department. Elmer E. Sherwood was the chief of the combined department and Harry S. O'Dell assistant chief, serving until the paid department was established in 1905. Andrew J. Land would then be chief with Lafe W. Moore as assistant chief.

The apparatus of the new Bellingham paid department was carried over from the brigades. Their apparatus included a modern three horse combination hose and chemical wagon. This boasted a single sixty-gallon chemical tank to pressurize a small hose reel, and carried 1,200 feet of hose. BFD also inherited a two-horse hose wagon with 1,000 feet of hose. They also had a 5000' reserve supply of new cotton jacketed hose, as well as 4000' feet of old, heavy rubber hose. The six hand-drawn hose carts from the brigades were distributed in the residential sections, while the two-horse combination chemical wagon and the Bennett Silsby steam engine were held in reserve for big fires. BFD's original fully-paid staff consisted of twelve men who were on duty constantly. The career longevity of these firefighters was not what we enjoy today.

Pulling the Alarm

By Fire/EMS Dispatcher Cindy Sluys

In 1911, the public system for reporting fires and other emergencies worked handily, even if it wasn't as nifty as today's 911. Single-pull switches in free-standing metal boxes had been installed by the fire department at many major intersections and buildings throughout the city. The boxes rang into the dispatch switchboard in Fire Station 1 on Prospect Street, and were identified by number. Firefighters quickly learned the locations of the box numbers in their territories, but also had a list in the engine for reference.

Although telecommunications was brand-new at the time and the word itself hadn't even been coined, cutting-edge Bellingham had a telephone line in service for people to report emergencies from areas without call boxes, if they could find a phone. The number was Main 97. The telephone switchboard would connect people who requested this line to Station 1, and the dispatch could then proceed somewhat as it does today.

This reporting system of alarm boxes supplemented by rare calls to Main 97 was efficient for the time, in part because neither method was used very often. In 1912, BFD responded to 500 alarms from three stations, so the telephone line sat silent for long periods. Seeing a modern, new technology that was just sitting there anyway, opportunistic firefighters started using the emergency phone to place occasional personal calls. Sometimes family members would call, looking for a department member. In time, this personal use became a common practice, to the extent that citizens trying to place an emergency call for assistance often found the line busy.

In 1912, Fire Chief J.J. Marsh was forced to forbid department personnel from using Main 97 for personal calls. In the January 10, 1912 edition of The Fairhaven (newspaper), Chief Marsh pleaded with the public not to use Main 97 except to report an emergency.

We're told that citizens of the time failed to heed Chief Marsh, and some still miss his point today. Despite wide recognition of 911 as an emergency access number, despite fiber optic speed, instant caller address verification, computer aided dispatch coding, and a BFD call load of over 12,000 runs each year, inappropriate use continues. Fire dispatchers still answer calls from people who want directions, or want the time of day, or want to contact a firefighter they met in a tavern the night before.

BELLINGHAM FIRE ALARM BOXES

ALL FIRE HALL PHONES 97

21—Broadway and Holly.
22—Eldridge and Henry.
23—F and Holly.
24—Jaeger and Monroe.
25 Halleck (21st) and G.
27—Park and Monroe
28—E and Dupont (17th).
29—Eldridge and Keesling
31—C and Holly.
32—Loggie's Mill.
33—C and Halleck (21st).
34—Ellis and North.
35—Kearney (24th) and G
36—Humboldt and North.
37—Monroe and Meridian.
38—C and Logan.
39—Elk and James.
41—Morrison Mill.

42—Virginia and Ellis.
43—Prospect St Fire Hall.
45—Bay and Holly.
47—Dock and Holly.
51—Elk and East Holly.
52—St. Joseph's Hopital.
53—Maple and Elk.
54—Elk and Rose.
57—Elk and Pine.
58—Garden and Pine.
61—B. B. I. Co. Mill.
63—Garden and Maple.
64—Maple and Indian.
65—Maple Ellis and Mason
68—East Holly and High.
71—Lake and Holly.
73—Potter and Grant.
75—Champion and Humboldt.
78—Royal Dairy Products Co.

SOUTH SIDE ALARMS.

123—Eleventh and Bennett.
124—E. K. Wood Mill.
125—Fourteenth and So. Elk.
126—Sixth and Harris.
132—Ninth and Harris.
134—Eleventh and Harris.
141—Twelfth and Knox.
143—Twelfth and Donovan.
152—Sixteenth and Harris.
154—Twenty-first and Harris
163—Fourteenth and Douglas.
168—Sixteenth and Knox.

111—One Company Call

222—General Alarm

Compliments of

5 to 8 Am FAIRHAVEN PHARMACY 6 to 9 PM

G. E. FINNEGAN

1209 ELEVENTH STREET PHONE 611

(OVER)

Provided by Gordon Tweit

1989.27.96 Whatcom Museum

Dressed in their finest uniforms, several fire companies parade up a narrow wood-planked Holly Street, past the intersection with Railroad Avenue, in what was then called the town of Sehome. Firemen easily outnumber the spectators at this event.

Mike Larson Collection

Men and equipment of the Cosgrove Hose Company No. 2 are dressed for the parade.

1996.10.442 Biery Collection-Whatcom Museum

A dozen members of the Sehome Hose Company visit a portrait studio. The date, and their reason for this apparel, are unknown.

1996.10.2394 Biery Collection-Whatcom Museum

The hats identify these men as members of the Cosgrove Hose Company. The breast plates and belt buckles declare, without question, that it's Company No. 2. Their namesake and sponsor, Edmund Cosgrove, was the first mayor of New Whatcom.

1996.10.2383 Biery Collection-Whatcom Museum

Within the Cosgrove Hose Company No. 2, rank had its privileges, like a great big badge, or a distinctive white belt, or a giant white Chief's helmet. Some men were involved in both the fire service and law enforcement, which probably enlarged the size of their badge considerably.

1977.41.4 Whatcom Museum

The Cosgrove Hose Company was organized in 1890. Here they appear in "Volunteers on Parade" along wooden Elk Street (now State Street), between Chestnut and Holly Streets, in what was then the town of New Whatcom, on July 4, 1892.

1989.27.2 Whatcom Museum

There's no mistaking the members of Cosgrove Hose Company No. 2, as they stand proudly on the steps of the New Whatcom City Hall (now the Whatcom Museum of History and Art).

1996.10.443 Biery Collection-Whatcom Museum

Chester I. Camp was born on April Fools Day, 1884, in Slate Creek, Kansas, and arrived here in 1900. He joined the Sehome Hose Company No. 1 on February 6, 1903, and was active until the group disbanded a year later. By October of 1904 he was "connected with the paid department," and served as a driver on Chemical Wagon #1.

Mike Larson Collection

Wardner Hose Company No. 2 at the Donovan Avenue fire hall before horses were enlisted to pull the equipment.

1977.41.7 Whatcom Museum

Dressed in their best parade uniforms, members of Warner Hose Company No. 2 pause for a portrait in front of their Donovan Avenue station. An inscription on the back of the photo reads, "Presented to Miss Olive Larson by Captain J.H. Mulrein, Dec. 10, 1890."

1977.41.5 Whatcom Museum

A sense of folded-arm defiance is displayed by Wardner Hose Company No. 2, circa 1890. A mysterious "Notice" has been glued to every door of the station behind them.

1977.41.6 Whatcom Museum

Hegg's Photo Studio, seen in the background, probably took this photo. The horse-drawn parade float of the Pioneer Hook and Ladder Company No. 1 features a doll being saved from the upper balcony of a miniature house. Organized in August 7, 1889, and then for some reason reorganized on May 9, 1890, the company's motto was "Ready for Duty." In April of 1893 the company claimed to have 20 members, and boasted that they "...never failed to report promptly when its services have been needed..." with "...a record to date of thirty-one responses to alarms."

x.4568.1 Whatcom Museum

Over twenty members of the Pioneer Hook and Ladder Company No. 1 prepare to pull their wagon in a Fourth of July parade on Elk Street, near where the Orchard Terrace buildings stand today.

1989.27.111 Whatcom Museum

It would appear that Pioneer Hook and Ladder Company No. 1 allowed individual expression through one's choice of neckwear, but the mustache formula was strictly enforced. c. 1893.

1996.10.516 Whatcom Museum

John J. Marsh was Assistant Chief for the City of Whatcom when this portrait was taken in 1902. He later served as BFD's Chief from 1909 to 1914, and again from 1916 to 1917.

Mike Larson Collection

A 1902 booklet discovered by chance at a Buckley, Washington, flea market provided what may be the only surviving images of these three groups. This one is the Whatcom Hook and Ladder Company No. 2.

Mike Larson Collection

Whatcom Hose Company No.3.

Mike Larson Collection

Whatcom Hose Company No. 4.

1989.27.117 Whatcom Museum

Sehome Hose Company No. 1 was organized March 26, 1890. By January 25, 1892 the company claimed to have "…responded to 25 alarms of fire…" and "…one hose cart and 900 feet of hose under its entire care and supervision…". They boasted of three officers and "…18 active members, of whom none are laggards, but are ever ready and watching to protect our glorious city from the destructive demon, fire." Circa 1900.

1996.10.489 Biery Collection-Whatcom Museum

Charlie Hofercamp, the young fellow seen here in the middle of Sehome Hose Company No. 1, was the group's "Lantern Boy." The precise nature of his duties remains unknown. The company's motto was "Deeds, Not Words."

Center for Pacific NW Studies # 777

Whatcom Hose Company No. 1 (formerly Sehome Hose #1) gather in front of their Forest Street station, circa 1902.

79.57.165 Whatcom Museum

Sehome Hose Company No. 1 assemble at the curb with their hose cart, while the Cosgrove Hose Company No. 2 look on from the rear. This early station, with its lofty bell tower, dominated Chestnut Street, where Cap Hanson's tavern stands today. One member of the Pioneer Hook and Ladder Company clings to his rig in the open doorway, and points to something in the distance. Circa 1890.

FACILITIES

Home Away From Home...

By Fire/EMS Dispatcher Toni Carpenter

For the fourteen years preceding the formation of Bellingham Fire Department, numerous volunteer companies were organized and sponsored by prominent citizens who pitched in for equipment and uniforms. These companies were quartered in existing or remodeled structures that could accommodate their apparatus.

One such building was the City of Fairhaven City Hall that housed Fairhaven Hook and Ladder Co.#1. In 1891, this station had a paid Engineer and 60 volunteer members. A committee was appointed to procure and install a tub bath and shower at a cost not to exceed $80, as well as athletic equipment for $30. In 1896, the Dock Street Company installed a bathtub in their hall after a year of strenuous effort securing that luxurious fixture!

In 1904, Bellingham Fire Department was founded. The property owners and progressive citizens of Bellingham brought about the movement to change the fire service from volunteers to paid personnel who would dutifully give the business of fighting fires their undivided attention. Fire Headquarters at Station 1 was located at 201 Prospect (current site of the Whatcom Museum's Syre Education Center). This station came to be known as the North Side, with the fire hall at 1112 Donovan called the South Side.

Built on land that was actually a street, Station 1 was 52 x 41 feet and two stories high. The building was brick veneered and had two 12 foot electrically operated doors that opened onto the street, a wonder of modern technology. One door was wide enough for two rigs to exit, allowing three rigs to leave the station at the same time. On the first floor of the station there were seven stalls: six for regular fire horses and one for the Chief's horse. The horses were trained to automatically walk under their harnesses suspended from the ceiling when the fire bell sounded. The truck room had ample space for three wagons. In the rear of the first floor was a 52-foot tower. Ventilation of the station was accomplished through the tower so no odor from the horses would be noticeable by the crews upstairs.

On the second floor of the station were an upstairs sitting room, and a dormitory with two brass poles for rapid decent to the lower level. Also on the second floor were the Chief's office, the electric-wired alarm room and a bathroom with all the modern conveniences.

On November 8, 1908, BFD commissioned Station 3 at Indian and Maple St. The original station faced Maple St. and was hailed as one of the best buildings of its kind in the Northwest. It measured 40x62 feet and had a company of four firemen. It boasted cozy quarters for the men and as many, if not more, conveniences than were found in the city's other fire halls.

Station 3 acquired its famous Spanish stucco exterior motif in 1928, then remained largely unchanged until it was demolished and rebuilt on the same site in 1984 facing Indian St. The new, much larger structure, almost 9000 square feet, was designed for a crew of eight. In 1988, the station was remodeled, then 10 years later needed a more extensive redesign due to ongoing problems in the original construction. This station is home to Engine 53, Ladder 41, Rescue 91, and Metro the Station Kitty, who has more seniority than most of the crew assigned there.

In 1926 and 1927, BFD commissioned two new stations and rebuilt Station 1. The original Station 1 was torn down. The new design included a communications center that could receive single alarms from pull stations. In 1955, a small single-story addition for a modern telephone dispatch center was built at this same station. It had its own separate entrance and a wonderful view.

The first new station built in 1926/27 was at East North and Vallette Streets. It was intended to be the department's new Station 4. The station opened New Year's Day 1928 with a three-person crew. Fire crews only occupied it briefly, until budget constraints forced its closure. The building was used as a Knights of Columbus Hall and polling place for some years before being torn down. Bellingham waited more than 30 years to open another fourth fire hall.

The second station built in 1926/27 was on 14th St. and Harris Ave. in Fairhaven. At a cost of $15,000, the new South Side fire hall could accommodate a crew of six along with a Seagrave combination and an antiquated steamer, which was held in reserve. Station 2 remained little changed until 2000 when it was decommissioned and operations were moved up the street to 1590 Harris Ave. Designed for a crew of six, this new station is 8,392 square feet and boasts a heated apparatus bay. The site acquisition was $622,031.73 and the design, construction and contents were $1,712,722.67! In 2003, the old hall at 14th and Harris was surplused to the private sector. Station 2 houses Engine 52, Medic/Aid 52, and HazMat 99.

Bellingham succeeded in opening a Station 4 again in

1960. Located on the corner of Iron and Alabama Street (620 Alabama), the BFD finally had a training tower and classroom. Twenty-eight years later, with the city expanding eastward, a new Station 4 was built at 2306 Yew St. With 8,320 square feet and quarters for six, this hall houses Engine and Aid 54.

In 1989, the old Station 4 became What-Comm Communications. It is now the primary answering point (PSAP) for 911 calls from Bellingham and most of Whatcom County. Calls for the cities of Blaine, Lynden and Sumas are handled by the US Border Patrol. From 1989 until the split between Fire and Police dispatching in 1999, What-Comm also housed Prospect fire dispatch. BFD still uses the training center and tower at this location today.

In 1971, a fifth station was added to the department at 3314 Northwest Ave. This tiny station underwent several remodels and expansions from 1974 to 1994. It is the smallest active BFD station, at only 4,864 square feet. Station 5 houses Engine 55, Medic/Aid 55, and HazMat 98.

BFD Headquarters acquired new digs at 1800 Broadway in 1990. It became the largest Bellingham station with 24,658 square feet for crew quarters (up to 11 crew), a five apparatus bay and BFD administrative offices. In 1999, Station 1 was reconfigured to hold the new Prospect Communications Center. At a cost of $73,000 plus computer dispatch equipment, Prospect became a dedicated Fire/EMS dispatch center once again. Station 1 houses Engine and Aid 51, Medic 1, Medic 2, Battalion 1 and the Arson van.

In 1990, with calls for medical service increasing in the county, BFD's Whatcom Medic One program installed a manufactured home at 1886 Grandview Road for Medic 3's two paramedics. The property, owned by Whatcom County Fire District 7, also houses District 7's volunteer-staffed Enterprise Station. Medic 3's manufactured home was replaced with a new manufactured home in 2003 at a cost of $115,261.

After acquiring property at 4060 Deemer Rd. for $125,000, BFD commissioned Station 6 in 2002. Construction of the new hall cost $1,358,044 and was funded by a $2.8 million bond issue in 2001. At 8,954 square feet, the contents of this station cost $100,000; the new fire engine was $450,000. New radios and equipment cost $50,000 – a far cry from Fairhaven Hook and Ladder's $80 bathtub. This station houses Engine and Medic/Aid 56.

Seeing a need for another medic unit to cover the East County, the Medic One program in 2002 commissioned another station at 858 E. Smith Rd. for Medic 4 and its two medics. This existing home was purchased and refurbished for $295,000.

Over the years, billiard tables have been replaced by stair-stepper machines, tub baths by showers, brass poles by stairs, and horses by shiny red fire engines. The one thing that has not changed is that the fire "laddies" and "lassies," with all the modern conveniences of home, continue a tradition of dutifully giving their undivided attention to the business of fighting fires and aiding those in need.

x.4565.1 Biery Collection-Whatcom Museum

When Fairhaven consolidated with Whatcom to form the new City of Bellingham, the old Fairhaven City Hall and jail building was transformed into Bellingham's second fire station. It was located at 1112 Donovan, but later gave way to commercial development. The building is seen here in an April, 1952 photo by Galen Biery.

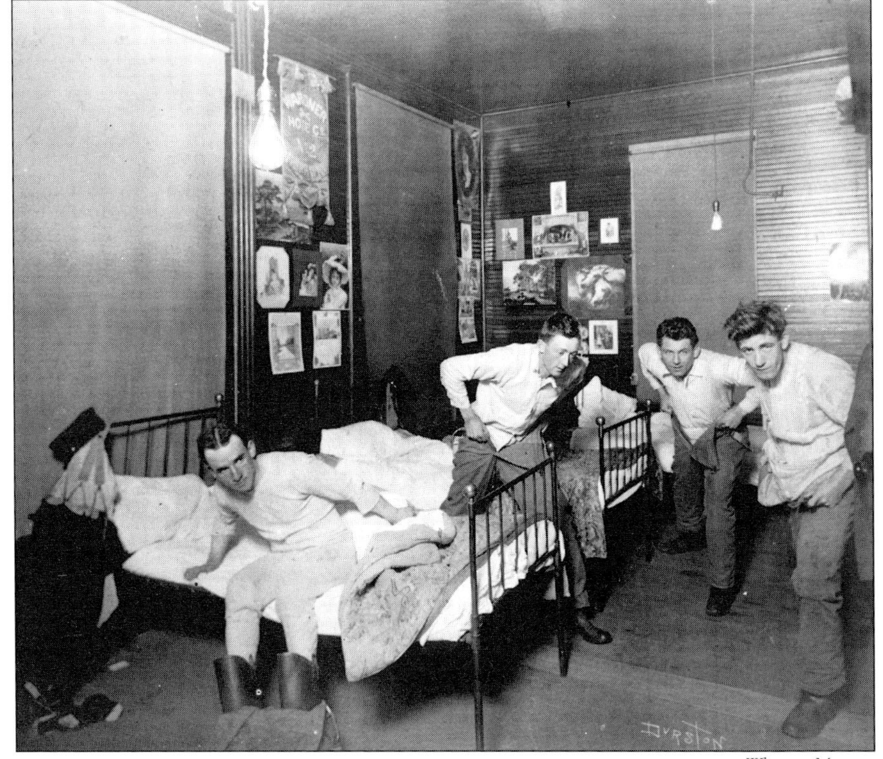

Whatcom Museum

Bare bulbs light the dorm room at Station 2 on Donovan Avenue. The walls are decorated with photos of fires, horses, and women. Someone has preserved the old Wardner Hose Company banner, too.

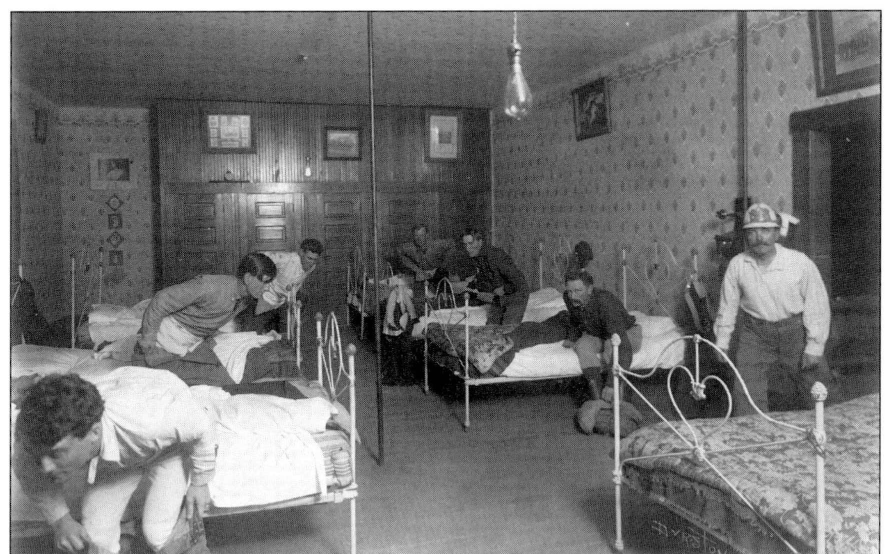

Tim Marsh Collection

Staged for the camera, this crew at old Station #1 on Prospect Street demonstrates a middle-of-the-night response.

x4059.1 Whatcom Museum

Although used very infrequently these days, this pool table now resides at Fire Station #3, protected for its sentimental and historic value. It has survived one total reconstruction and several extensive remodeling projects at Station #3, and now "rolls true."

1996.10.2380 Biery Collection-Whatcom Museum

The wallpaper may have been a distraction, but games were played and meetings were held in this second floor room at the original Propsect Street Station #1, seen here about 1910.

1996.10.2401 Biery Collection-Whatcom Museum

Around 1910, recreation opportunities at the Donovan Avenue Station #2 included games of skill, games of chance, and pugilism practice.

4190A Sandison Collection- Whatcom Museum

In the rear of the old Station #1 on Prospect Street was hidden the "alarm room", which connected to dozens of call boxes scattered around the City and controlled all BFD dispatch operations.

1996.10.51.3 Biery Collection-Whatcom Museum

In 1905, BFD electrician G.L. Crews maintained the Gamewell fire alarm telegraph switchboard, located in the rear of Station #1 on Prospect Street.

2003.10.21 The Bellingham Herald's Jack Carver Collection – Whatcom Museum

In this July 26, 1955 meeting, Chief Mike Mohl, electrician DeWitt Dunhaver, and Bob Messick (assigned to the "Command Desk") contemplate moving the fire department's call-receiving and dispatch center to a new location. The perforated paper tape and brass bells would eventually make way for more modern equipment.

BFD Archives

"Prospect" became forever synonymous with BFD dispatch facilities because they were located for so many years at the rear of Station #1 on Prospect Street. Although today's Bellingham fire and County-wide EMS dispatch is located elsewhere, it still goes by the "Prospect" moniker.

1980.74.102 Whatcom Museum

Built in 1927 on the extreme northern fringe of the developed city (East North and Vallette Streets), this fire station was designed by F. Stanley Piper. The site measured 100' by 100', and was purchased for $715 in 1926. Conceived and built almost simultaneously with new Station 2 at 14th and Harris on the opposite end of town, this station fell victim to the stock market crash and Great Depression. Declines in local tax revenues closed the station permanently on December 31, 1934. It was eventually sold, converted to a duplex, and finally demolished to make way for new development as the city expanded. Its "sister" station #2 in Happy Valley was fully staffed and operational for 73 years.

4079 Sandison Collection-Whatcom Museum

At the southwest corner of 14th Street and Harris Avenue, Station #2 was commissioned on June 30, 1927. Built at a cost of $15,000, on property Cirus Gates sold to the City for $1, the station was active for seventy-three years until replaced in 2000. The original twin hinged folding doors were adequate for apparatus of the day, but were eventually replaced with a single overhead door when apparatus grew too wide to negotiate the narrow openings. Today, an active fireplace seems to be an odd element to include in a fire station. The property was sold to a private owner in 2003.

1995.1 The Bellingham Herald's Jack Carver Collection – Whatcom Museum

Frequent renovations tried to keep Station #2 current. As apparatus grew larger and wider, the original two hinged doors gave way to a single overhead door seen here in 1972.

DAILY REPORT OF FIRES IN June And July 1914																				
				Names of Parties Sustaining Loss		Kind of Building and Occupancy Number of Stories—Brick, Stone, Concrete, Iron-Clad or Frame				Fires					Extinguished By					
Date	Time	Alarm Box Telephone, Still or False	Location	Owner of Building	Occupant	No. of Stories	Kind of Build'g	Occupancy	Fires other than in Buildings Grass, Dump, Fences, Bridges, Cars, Lumber, etc.	Confined to Floor	Confined to Build'g	Extending to Adj'ng Bldgs.	Extending Beyond Adj'ng Bldgs.	Cause	Out on Arrival	Citizens or Empl's only	Automatic Sprinklers	Chemicals—Gals. Used	No. of Hose Streams Used	Engines Working
May 26	2.20 Am	Telephone	1004. 12 St	H.M. Koebler	L.N. Johnson	Two	Wood	Residence			yes			From. Adj'ng. Bldg					3	1600
May 26	2.20 Am	Telephone	1006. 12 St	J.L. Gazley	H.L Fuller	Two	Wood	Residence				yes		Overheated Stove						
May 26	2.20 Am	Telephone	1008. 12 St	J.L. Gazley	J.L. Gazley	Three	Wood	Residence			yes			From Adj'ng Bldg						
May 27	12.10 Am	Telephone	1315 Dock St			Two	Brick	Bakery						Smoke From Furnace						
May 30	2.5 Am	Box 31	709½ W. Holly			Two	Wood													
June 16	9.55 Pm	Box 35	G & Kerney							yes				Smokeing. In Bed						
June 18	8.28 Am	Box 54	Elk & Rose											False						
June 18	8.53 Am	Box 143		Earles Cleary		One	Wood							False Boy Mail Letter						
June 20	11.50 Am	Telephone	1200 Elk St	W Slade	J J Graham	Two	Wood	Dye Works		yes				Blow out From Boiler						500
June 20	8 50 Pm	Box 154	Donavon St	Pease		Two	Wood	Residence			yes			Gasolene Explosing					20	550
June 22	7.20 Pm	Phone	N.P. Depot	N.P Ry						yes				Incendiarism					6	
June 30	10. Pm	Box 33	C. & Halleck						Box Car	yes				Incendiarism					20	
July 3	10.25 Pm	Box 141	12th & Knox											False						
July 4	12.10 Pm	Box 45	305. W. Holly		Carstens Co.	Two	Wood	Meat Market						False						
July 4	1.17 Pm	Phone	1204½ Indian St	H.W. Buzzard	R. Buzzard	One	Wood	Residence						Ammonia Tank						
July 4	6.25 Pm	Phone	509. W. Holly St	McLain		One	Wood	Store						Firecrackers						
July 4	11.45 Pm	Box 53	Maple & Elk											Fire Crackers						
July 5	9.45 Am	Still	Adams. & S. Elk											False						
July 5	6.40 Pm	Box 47	201 E. Holly		Frye & Co.	Two	Brick	Meat Market						Fire in Plank						
July 8	8. Pm	Phone	2616 Peabody. St	M Langley		Two	Wood	Residence		yes				Pipe Droped in Awning						
July 11	1.35 Pm	Phone	800 Garden, St			One	Wood	Shed		yes				Unknown					3	
July 13	10.20 Pm	Phone	Lottie & Grand Ave											Fire Crackers						
July 15	2.15 Pm	Box 37	2900. Kulshan. St											Rubbish						300
July 16	2.25 Pm	Phone	Carolina & Queen	Mrs W. Hewitt	L. Reymer	One	Wood	Residence						Grass						
July 16	3.05 Pm	Box 154	1201. 22nd St.	M.S. Brownridge		One	Wood	Barn		yes				Incendiarism						800
July 17	10.15 Am	Phone	711 Carolina St	K. Sauset		One	Wood	Wood Shed		yes				Unknown					20	
July 17	12.40 Pm	Phone	2900 Blk Kulshan								yes			Unknown					20	300
July 18	11.55 Am	Phone	119. W. Holly St	Otto Schleuder	W.A. Hall	Two	Wood	Store		yes				Grass						
July 21	4.45 Am	Phone	Silver Beach	Mrs A.A. Goodell		One	Wood	Residence		yes				Cigar Lighter						
														Unknown						

BFD Archives

A page from Station #1's log book, May 26 through July 21, 1914. In the Cause column, "False Boy Mail Letter" meant someone tried to mail a letter via a fire alarm call box. "Incendiarism" is a curious entry, too.

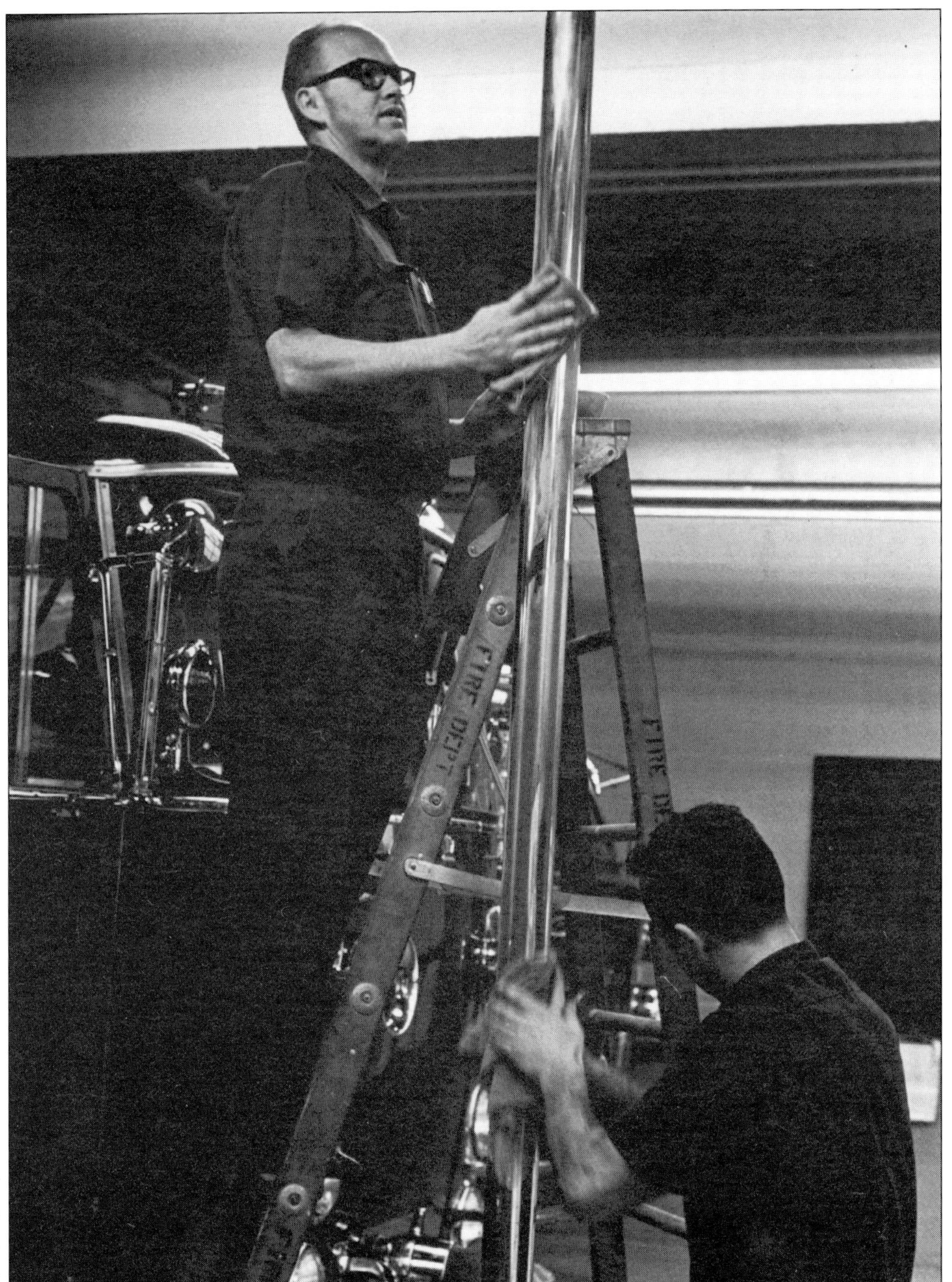

1989.27.158c Whatcom Museum

The brass pole became a fire station icon, providing quick descent from upper levels of multi-story stations, like this one at the Prospect Street Station #1. Some large stations in major urban settings would have several poles, used to descend from the upper floors. Injuries eventually lead to industrial insurance regulations that spelled the end of the brass pole tradition.

X5023.1 Whatcom Museum

Clean white shirts are the order of the day for the scaling and rappelling exercises on the east (Indian Street) side of original Station #3.

1996.10.511 Biery Collection-Whatcom Museum

The original Station #3, at East Maple and Indian Streets received this Spanish stucco exterior when remodeled in 1928. There were rumors that one of the BFD horses had been buried on the site. It was replaced with a new structure on the same site in 1984.

Alabama Street was still quite narrow when Chief Wes Baker officially opened the original Station #4 on February 3, 1960, with the La France Engine No. 3 on display. The station was later relocated to 2306 Yew Street in 1988, and this structure was remodeled to became the What-Comm 911 dispatch center.

2003.10.014 The Bellingham Herald's Jack Carver Collection – Whatcom Museum

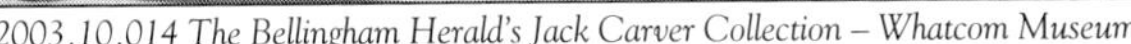

1995.1 The Bellingham Herald's Jack Carver Collection – Whatcom Museum

Seen here in 1971, this second generation Station #1 at 201 Prospect Street replaced the previous facility on the same site. Today it's the home of the Syre Education Center of the Whatcom Museum of History and Art.

1989.27.135 Sandison Collection-Whatcom Museum

With the Great Depression in full swing, twenty-seven Bellingham fire fighters organized a BFD band February 20, 1930.

THE PEOPLE

Colorful Commrades...

Pressure, tragedy, exhilaration, and fear. A firefighter's day can suddenly transform into an intense mix of emotions. Placing their trust, and sometimes their lives, in the hands of others, its little wonder that firefighters build a rapport and a bond unknown in most other lines of work.

The station is their second home, twenty-four hours at a stretch. They work, eat, sleep, train, and play together, learning each other's hobbies, habits, and humor. And the bond builds.

Good-natured pranks and a little ribbing help to break the ice, and break the tension. Firehouse stories are legendary, growing with each retelling, taking on a zest that may not have been part of the original event. Perhaps a sampling of those stories, whether entirely true or not, can provide a peek into the core of BFD's most important asset...the people.

Flowers & Onions

By Fire/EMS Dispatcher Toni Carpenter

In the 1930's, landscaping at Station #3 was rather stark. But firefighter Ray Moblo was determined to brighten things up.

Ray spent considerable time working the soil along the Indian St. side of the newly rebuilt fire hall. This ground had never been tended, other than having the grass cut. Ray removed the wild-growing grass, plucked the weeds and carted off loads of rocks. The soil had to be mulched and fertilized, too. That was just the kind of hardworking firefighter Ray was. Soon the soil was ready, and Ray planted dozens of tulip bulbs.

During the cold, dark winter months, Ray checked persistently on his precious bulbs, covering, uncovering, making sure they were ok, anxious for the colors of spring.

Finally the little green shoots appeared. Ray continued to care for them as they grew. As time went on, though, he noticed something odd about the plants. When no flower buds appeared on the mature stalks, he became concerned. Then Ray got a whiff of the truth: his tulips were really onions!

You see, not only was Ray a hardworking guy, but so were his fellow firefighters. On all those grey days they had matched Ray's work bulb for bulb, replacing tulips with onions.

Not To Be Denied

By Fire Inspector Don Davis

In the early sixties, the "pipeman," or "nozzleman," rode to fires standing on the engine's tailboard. On this particular day, the pipeman at Station 3 was a motivated firefighter named Ole Olson. He was chatting with a motorcycle cop who had stopped by.

The fire bell rang and Engine 3 was dispatched to a fire at a mill on the Southside. Moments later, as the engine rumbled down the steep Maple St. hill, the captain glanced over his shoulder to check on his pipeman – and didn't see him! "I think Ole fell off!" he yelled over the engine noise.

"What should we do?" the driver yelled back.

"Keep going!" And so they did.

Ole hadn't fallen off the engine at all. He hadn't even gotten on. He simply hadn't had time to bunker up and climb aboard before the hotfoot driver pulled away.

The engine was racing down State Street when a motorcycle cop passed it with a firefighter clinging to his back, bunker coat flapping in the wind. "That's Ole!" yelled the captain, as relieved as he was surprised. The cop got a good lead on the fire engine, then pulled over and stopped. Engine 3 slowed, the pipeman hopped onto the tailboard, and off they went to fight the fire.

That sort of resourceful persistence would eventually earn Ole Olson the rank of Battalion Chief.

With an array of prominent brass accessories displayed, James L. Odell strikes a direct pose at a local portrait studio, circa 1916.

Mike Larson Collection

'60s Conflict

By Battalion Chief Don Beattie

Nobody said it would be easy. Emergency work and the 24-hour shift define who people are and affect and how they relate to each other. This can lead to tight teams, esprit de corps and great camaraderie.... the best of times. It can also lead to tension and dissention....the worst of times. And, that is where the pendulum swung during the 1960's when the union (Local 106 of the International Association of Fire Fighters) and the administration clashed. A division was drawn and the department was ripped in half.

There was no single trigger to the falling out. City policies provided nearly unchecked disciplinary power to the Fire Chief. Local 106 sought to change that. Fire fighters were suspended without pay for union activities. Local 106 attempted to reverse those suspensions. There was distrust of the promotional process. Local 106 proposed a system of "Seniority with Ability" for promotions. Leave time was at times awarded inconsistently and unfairly and assignments were sometimes seen as a means of retribution or punishment. Local 106 wanted a standard system based on seniority and consistency and fairness.

Local 106 was defining its role. Many fire fighters were veterans of the military in WWII and Korea. Some found retooling their military way of thinking to unionism was difficult, or even wrong. In addition, fire fighters were mostly local. Members knew each other. They were neighbors who grew up and attended school together. Some were friends, or enemies, long before they worked together in the BFD.

During the years between 1958 and 1966 the union and the administration fought bitterly. Personalities clashed. A group of 24 union members withdrew from Local 106 and formed the Bellingham Fire Fighters Association to support the chief, to support the right to suspend without cause (with no chance for appeal) and to support the promotional practices of the day. The battle was fought openly on the pages of the Bellingham Herald, and in meeting reports of the Civil Service Commission.

Changes were finally enacted in 1966, after a formal Civil Service Commission investigation of the Fire Department and its practices. The authority of the chief to discipline was trimmed. Leave time procedures were made standard. The issue of "Seniority with Ability" promotions went to the voters and passed but was written out of a new city charter within a year.

The department moved slowly toward unification. The Association disbanded and most of the Association members, but not all, rejoined the Union. Some wounds healed with time. Others never did.

The two sides of the issues were neither absolutely right nor absolutely wrong. One stood on solid labor principles, the other on order and allegiance. Individual stake and personal interest contributed to distorted perception and detoured reason. Seeking a rational solution to an impasse is always best, but it is not always easy. Regardless of who believed what, the issues needed resolving. Many of the benefits city employees enjoy today were earned through the efforts of Local 106 in the 60's.

Firony

By Fire Inspector Don Davis

Way back when, "Stinky" Davis lived in the Bank Apartments at 11th and Harris in Fairhaven. Stinky had had a traumatic experience with fire when he was a kid. He had been deathly afraid of fire ever since.

One night he woke to the cries of "Fire! Fire!" Without hesitation Stinky bolted from his room, ran down the hall in his underwear, and jumped from the outside stair landing.

The fire was small, limited to a smoldering mattress. The firefighters dragged the mattress down the hall and threw it outside. A few minutes later, as they were loading their tools back on their engine, the firefighters heard muffled cries for help. After several minutes of searching, they found the person in distress.

Yup, it was Stinky, buried deep in a blackberry thicket, leg broken, and pinned by the smoldering mattress.

A. M. MUIR, MAYOR

The City of Bellingham
Fire Department
Bellingham, Washington

J. J. MARSH, CHIEF
BERT SYBRANT, ASSISTANT

May 22,1917.

George C Main

Seattle Wash.

Dear Sir:

You said that never again,when you did not send the los on the Clover Block but I see that the little less on the Alaska building-ga- has sliped your mind and I trust that you will send it along at your first oppertunity .Thanking you for past fevors I beg to remain,

Yours truly

J. J. Marsh

Fire Chief.

Eighty-seven years ago, Chief Marsh (seen at the far right) authored this letter. Today's computer-based spell check feature would have been helpful.

Tim Marsh Collection

Chief John J. Marsh's badge. He held the post from 1909 to 1914, and again from 1916 to 1917.

Tim Marsh Collection

BFD Chief John J. Marsh presented a handsome profile. When he died in 1918 at the age of 48, the newspaper obituary credited him with "...sturdy parentage...inherent keenness for action...readiness of wit...a born mixer...", and related that he wanted to "...be found on duty when the time came for his passing on."

x4566.1 Whatcom Museum

Chief Frank Stearns (left) poses with BFD personnel ready for duty in WW I as "Dough Boys" and a sailor, in a group portrait with "Pat" the dog.

The "boys" in military uniform surround their BFD equipment. At left is a rare glimpse of the City's first ambulance. All new ambulance production was being routed to the war effort, so E.B. Deming, president of Pacific American Fisheries in Fairhaven, had this one built from hard wood (except the chassis and drive train) in his south side salmon cannery. He hired "...the best mechanics obtainable..." and made sure it carried "...every modern convenience known." He then donated it to the City. Circa 1918.

1981.36.99 Sandison Collection-Whatcom Museum

The Bellingham Herald's Jack Carver Collection – Whatcom Museum

With the country at war in 1943, BFD personnel assembled to show their military affiliations.

1980.74.105 Whatcom Museum

For a time, the property north of Station #1/Prospect was vacant and the occasional site of fire fighter recreation, circa 1920.

Sandison Collection – Whatcom Museum

Call box #64 adorns the wall of Old Station #3 as the crew strikes a stilted pose in 1909.

1995.1 The Bellingham Herald's Jack Carver Collection – Whatcom Museum

Santa arrived December 21, 1957, riding a fire truck along wide open Railroad Avenue, between Chestnut and Holly Streets. The Washington Grocery Building can be seen at the left rear.

1995.1.5.729 The Bellingham Herald's Jack Carver Collection – Whatcom Museum

Unlike the technique in this 1949 training exercise, today's fire fighters are taught to hold the hose, not the hose holder.

Photo provide by L.R. Gilfilen

A number of BFD fire fighters got facially involved in the beard growing contest during Blossomtime's festivities in May of 1953. Here they are joined by the Blossomtime Queen and her court, dressed for the occasion.

1989.27.142 Whatcom Museum

Fire Chief Wes Baker stands along side his 1956 Pontiac, an appropriate "Chieftain" model.

The Bellingham Herald's Jack Carver Collection – Whatcom Museum

High-ranking BFD personnel gathered for a photo January 29, 1959.

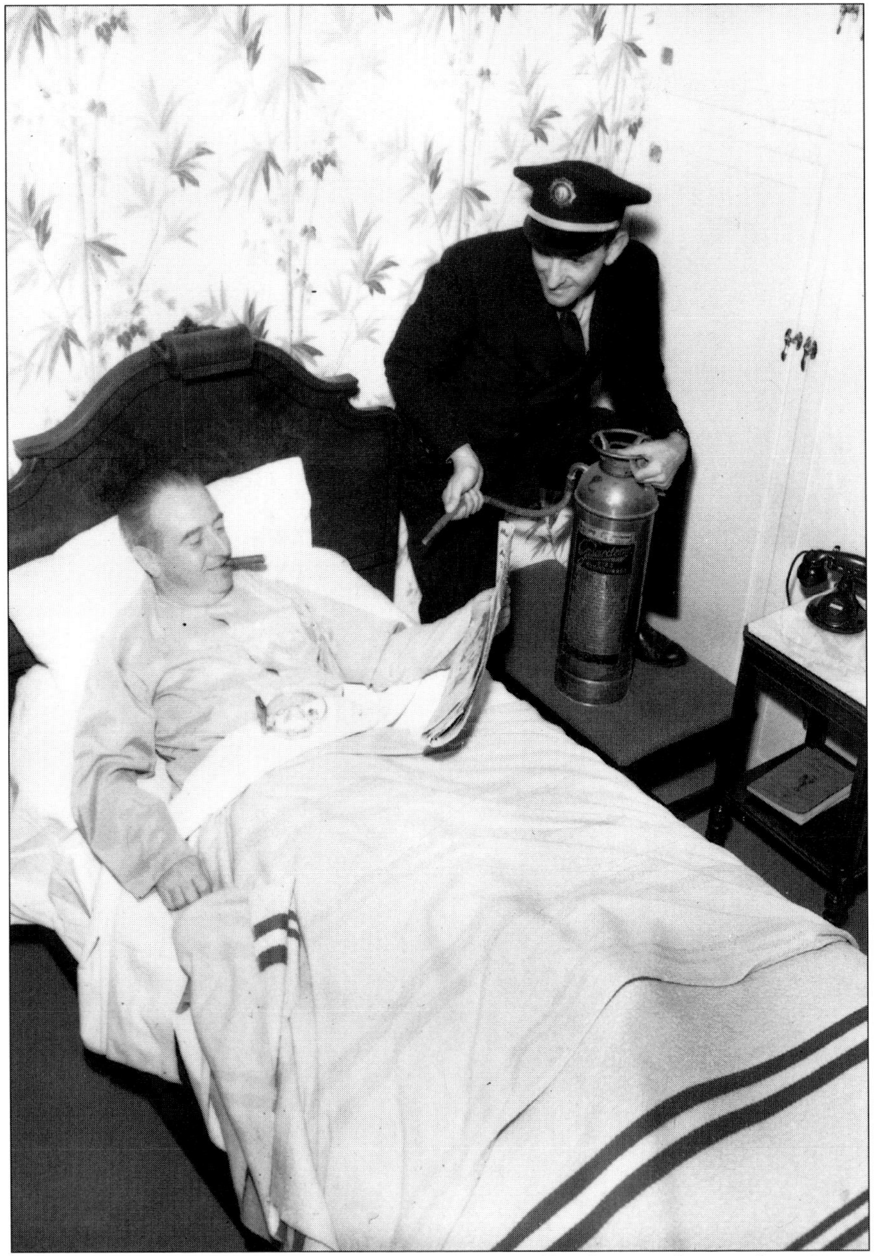

1995.1.5828 The Bellingham Herald's Jack Carver Collection – Whatcom Museum

John J. O'Rourke, manager of the Bellingham Hotel, and fire inspector Ralph Hennes gag it up for the "Don't Smoke In Bed" message during Fire Prevention Week in October 1950.

1995.1 The Bellingham Herald's Jack Carver Collection – Whatcom Museum

On September 17, 1954, Fire Chief Mike Mohl promotes Fire Prevention Week with a really swell slogan.

2003.10.22 The Bellingham Herald's Jack Carver Collection – Whatcom Museum

Blackboard penmanship and grammar seem to rival fire safety as the lesson-of-the-day while Dave Langford presents Junior Fire Marshal awards to shy 2nd or 3rd graders at Columbia school, on October 11, 1972.

2003.10.015 The Bellingham Herald's Jack Carver Collection – Whatcom Museum

Everyone's welcome to climb aboard during Kids Day at Station #1/Prospect on September 22, 1951.

1995.1 The Bellingham Herald's Jack Carver Collection – Whatcom Museum

The crew at Station #1/Prospect compare their modern rig to the giant wheels from an old hose cart.

1996.10.2375 Biery Collection-Whatcom Museum

The privilege of washing hose is usually reserved for the rookies.

1989.27.158d Whatcom Museum

A fire fighter works, sleeps, studies and eats at the fire house, his second home.

Photo provided by Ted Loney

While their turnouts are still clean, everyone gathers for a group picture moments before BFD fire fighters participate in messy flammable liquid fire training at the Cherry Point Arco refinery.

Photo provide by L.R. Gilfilen

Visiting a fire station can root some memories forever.

Photo provided by Brian Craven

After Brian Caven's first day on the job at BFD, his daughter Crystelle climbs into his turnout gear to check the fit.

Mike Larson Collection

In 1949, three-year-old Kenny Nelson and his five-year-old sister Mary lost their pet cocker spaniel "Curley" under the wheels of a BFD fire truck responding to a call. Two days later, fire fighters presented the kids with a new friend: a three-month old pup named "Curley II."

BFD Archives

Captain Chuck Henkel (left rear) and Captain Andy Day (far right) supervise a controlled practice burn for five new trainees at the end of their Recruit Academy in 2000. Day's wife brought their daughters by to watch daddy work, just as their school bus passed by. At school the next morning, Day's kids were flooded with condolences about their house burning down. The residence used in this exercise had coincidentally been the home of a BFD fire fighter some time before.

Photo provided by Ted Loney

In 1991, retired Captain Ted Loney (standing) commissioned Bellingham's Donnette Studio of Photography to create a family portrait. Son Brian (now with the Redmond Fire Department) is at the lower left. Son Bruce (now with the Bellevue Fire Department) holds the nozzle.

2003.10.012 The Bellingham Herald's Jack Carver Collection – Whatcom Museum

On September. 6, 1979, Leslie Lowrie, of Seattle, posted a time of 4 minutes, 02 seconds during applicant testing drills at the BFD training tower.

Photo provided by Ted Loney

These eight BFD fire fighters earned money for a charity when they volunteered for the humiliation of Donkey Basketball. One of them went on to eventually become Chief.

BFD Archives

Wherever they traveled around the state, BFD's 1970 slow pitch softball team struck absolute fear in the hearts of their fire department competitors. Or so they say.

Photo provided by Brian Craven

In 1993, BFD fire fighters assembled a team for the Over 40 Class in the annual Ski-to-Sea competition.

Metro & Mascots

By Fire/EMS Dispatcher Cindy Sluys

One of the first BFD mascots was "Rex," a Labrador or Mastiff weighing 70 to 80 pounds. In 1905 he would ride on the seat next to the driver of the combination hose/chemical engine from the Southside station.

After Rex, the firefighters wanted to train a seal to perform circus tricks. On August 30, 1909, a seal arrived, but it died within 24 hours. In 1915, Pete the bear became the Prospect station's pet and pride, a gift presented by local hunters. Pete passed on about a year later.

In the spring of 1989, a 6-month-old tabby kitty named Jim was living with some WWU students across the alley from Station 3 on Indian Street. Jim decided that the station was a pretty nice place, and moved in. About that time the Metro Dade County F.D. in Florida was in the news, so 3's crews started calling the cat "Metro." They attempted to return Metro to the students, but he kept coming back. Eventually, the students moved away, taking the cat. Everyone thought Metro was gone for good, but about a month later he returned, tired and skinny, never to leave again.

Metro has a BFD seniority number of 222.5. He has been through a station remodel, and a few health scares, but has bounced back each time. His fellow department members have been responsible for his health care, and probationers for holding the button on the water fountain so Metro can drink, until the invention in 2002 of the Metro auto-waterer, that is.

"Metro" adopted Station #3, not the other way around.

Photo by Martin Kink Jr.

Photo provided by Clayton Reed

His BFD keepers hold one of three bears that served in the role of department mascot at various times. The November 1, 1916 Bellingham Herald reported the death of "Pete, the ant bear...", which the department attributed to "lack of ants." Pete was, however, survived by "Peggy," a bear cub "...who has rivaled him in the affection of the department for the last few months."

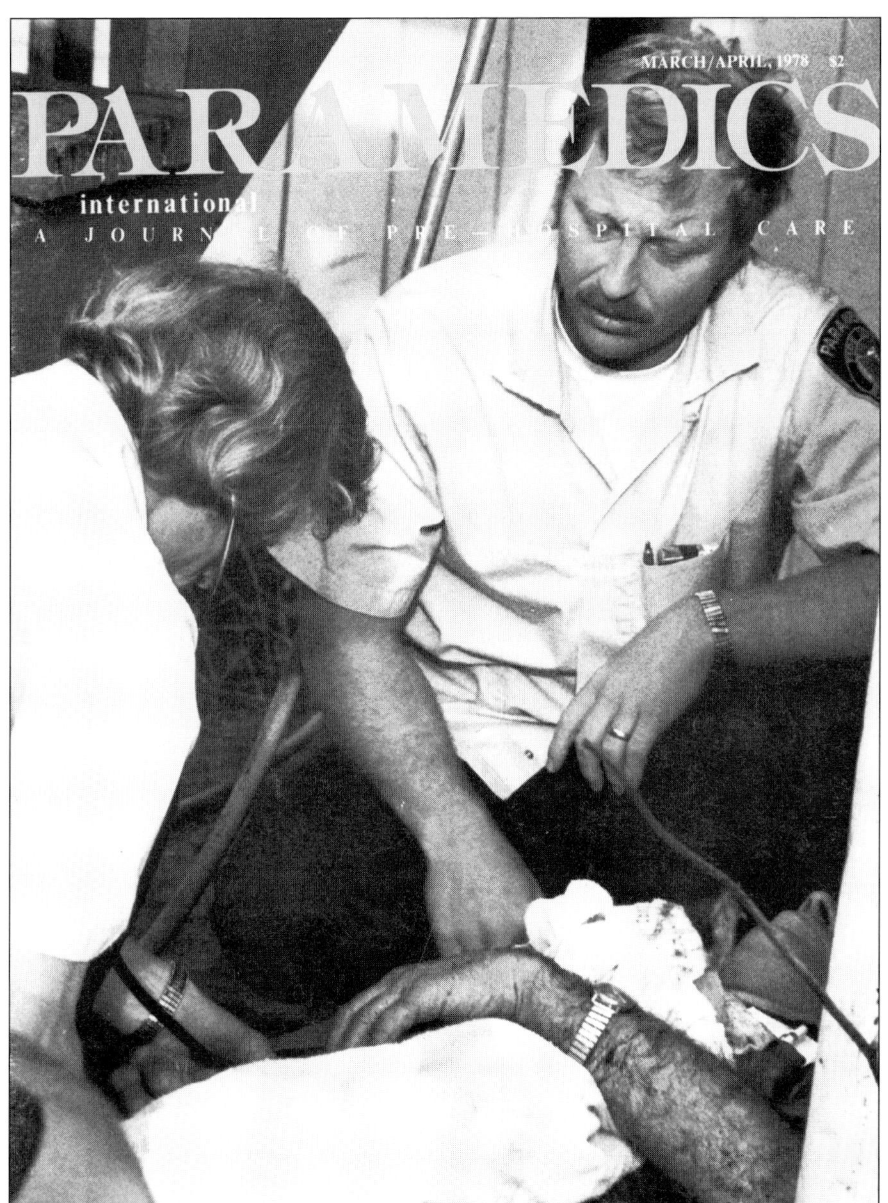

BFD Archives

BFD's struggles and successes in bringing about an exemplary EMS system were detailed in several trade journals during the late 1970s.

BFD Archives

Fourteen paramedics offered fourteen very different stories to explain the special equipment in this photo.

Tim Marsh Collection

A dozen hoofs, solid wood wheels, and a wood-planked street produced a thunderous announcement of this wagon's approach. The three-horse hitch and Combination Chemical Wagon #2 were racing south on 11th Street. Once they reached their destination, the horseman would disconnect the team and "cool" the horses by casually walking them around the neighborhood while the other fire fighters attacked the flames.

APPARATUS

And Equipment... The Tools Of The Trade

By Fire Fighter/Paramedic Sean Farnand

The machines and tools the Bellingham Fire Department has used to carry out its work have changed dramatically over its first century. While 2004 technology is dazzlingly more complex than our predecessors could have imagined, the goals that drive the changes remain consistent: get to the fire faster, get water on the fire faster and more effectively, save more lives and property, and do all these tasks more safely.

In the inaugural year of the BFD, the brand-new City of Bellingham stepped boldly into the 1900s by purchasing two new fire wagons equipped with a potent weapon for rapid fire extinguishment: chemical tanks. These sixty-gallon tanks worked on the same principle as handheld extinguishers of the day. A small quantity of sulfuric acid was mixed into the larger bicarbonate of soda reservoir by rotating the tank with a hand lever. The chemical reaction produced a lot of carbon dioxide, which pressurized the tank and rapidly charged a 200-foot hose reel of one inch hose for quick attack on a fire. The high CO2 content of this mixture was thought to smother fires better than water, and was certainly faster than rigging hoselines and hand pumps.

Unfortunately, the new combination chemical and hose wagons weighed 5500 pounds. Other hose or ladder wagons were much lighter and could be swiftly hauled over any terrain by two hardy horses. On the new apparatus' first day in service, rigged with only two horses, Chemical Engine 1 was thirty minutes late to a fire. The firefighters, now fully paid, arrived in time to watch the clean up work of volunteer companies who had passed them twenty minutes earlier, with many a kind word, going up Holly Street to the fire. The heavy rigs were soon changed to three horse hitches.

Firefighters loved their horses; they were family. The invention of the brass sliding pole and the pulley-guided, quick hitching Berry Hames and Collars allowed fire crews to be out the door minutes after the bell. By contrast, the earliest autos were undependable, noisy, and easily outraced by well-trained and experienced horse wagon crews.

Although horses were the early pride and mainstay of the unified BFD, new gas engines increasingly offered unarguable economies. After all, horses must eat whether they go to fires or not. In contrast, an auto that might only be expected to travel a few thousand miles in its service life ran on gasoline costing 10 to 12 cents per gallon.

In 1914, the Chief's Report lists the year's expenses for the horse-drawn combination wagon at Station 3 as $433.14, while the two new motor driven rigs together were only $231.32. Autos didn't need to be exercised, or cooled after an alarm; they didn't get ice balls on their hooves running through the snow, and smelly shoveling wasn't required. In the same report, Chief Hoffercamp called for the retirement of BFD's last horse team. Many old firefighters are said to have retired with their beloved horses rather than learn the new technology.

Putting water on the fire is just as important as getting there and is another area where fire service equipment has changed dramatically since 1904.

Piston driven pumps were common on early 1900's fire apparatus such as the BFD's Silsby steamer. These apparatus were identifiable by the large, shiny, pressure surge-reducing orb that sat atop the pumps. If the hose was shut down at the nozzle before the piston-driven pump was shut off, something had to break (hose or metal), because the pump couldn't run without displacing water at pressure.

In 1912, the Seagrave Company was overcoming this limitation of mechanical pumps by producing the first centrifugal pumps for fire apparatus. Driven by the rotational speed of the rig's engine, the pump's impeller could spin freely with ready water pressure even if the nozzle was shut down. These pumps are the standard for modern fire apparatus.

Also on their 1912 models, Seagrave introduced the pressure regulator, giving the engineer, for the first time, control of water pressure at the nozzle. These two innovations allowed tremendous flexibility and safety for nozzlemen and engineers alike. The BFD seized on the new ideas and bought two of the new Seagrave engines in their first year of production, overriding arguments that the technology was experimental.

For years, one of the most hotly debated features of fire apparatus in the department was the windshield. Many feared the glass could shatter while driving at breakneck speeds in excess of 25 mph, with terrible results. The 1930 White was the BFD's first with the worrisome glass. Crews quickly came to appreciate the improved visibility and warmth.

Despite three feet of annual rainfall, BFD firefighters would not know the luxury of an enclosed front cab until, in post-war exuberance, they bought a '49 Seagrave. Pipemen, however, were left standing, then sitting, backwards in the cold until the '97 Darleys.

The '30 White had another feature new to motorized apparatus, an 85-gallon on-board water tank. Horse wagons had carried water tanks in some cities years before, but water was plentiful in Bellingham. For the weak-willed early motor cars, carrying hose had been prioritized over carrying water. The development of 6 and 12-cylinder engines allowed apparatus to haul water, a pump, ladders and hose. The Quad was born.

As soon as fire apparatus were able to put cheap, clean water on fire quickly and efficiently, chemical tanks were no longer needed. BFD's '28 American LaFrance triple combo chemical hose pumper had a rotary pump rated at 750 gallons per minute, but their first weapon against fire remained the CO2. By 1949, the department's Seagrave boasted a 150-gallon water tank for quick attack, and a low-maintenance centrifugal pump that produced 1000 gpm at 120 psi.

Although the BFD has, historically, adopted new technologies quickly, it was relatively late in joining the move to diesel. The Stutz Motor Company marketed the first diesel fire engine in 1939. As the diesel motor's efficiency, durability and power were demonstrated, other manufacturers began to offer diesel engines too.

Fire departments today respond to many community needs and crises other than fire. Beginning in the 1950s, increased compartment space was required on fire engines to hold new tools and cutting-edge safety devices like self-contained breathing apparatus. Through the 60s and 70s, Bellingham's engines were larger than ever before. They required more power, and diesel began to make sense. The BFD fleet wasn't fully switched to diesel power until the early 80s.

BFD adopted a different nifty invention by Stutz early on. The '23 and '24 Stutz "pumping engines" featured headlights which, mounted low, were attached directly to the steering mechanism. When the driver turned a corner, the lights looked around the corner, too.

Indispensable for access and rescue, ladders have evolved through the century as well. The 1904 chemical wagons were equipped with two wood ladders which could be "connected quickly" to form a single 25-footer. Such a device was bound to fail under extreme fireground usage.

In 1914, the department's 30-foot wood extension ladders were deemed "wholly inadequate" for reaching upper floors. A request was made for a 65-foot, motor-driven hook and ladder, newly in production at the time.

By 1939, BFD had its first true aerial ladder truck, a state-of-the-art LaFrance/Foamite. Its metal ladder was lifted hydraulically, a new feature on LaFrance trucks. With that kind of power, Chief Ira T. Jones requested funding for a ladder pipe to be fitted to the new aerial, which allowed for effective extinguishment above the third floor.

Ladders, pumps, hose and axes, teamwork, brains, and guts: our work is still done with these tools. New devices that come along – like thermal imaging cameras or mobile data terminals – will be valuable to us so long as they aid in achieving our timeless goals: get to the fire, put water on the fire, save lives and property, and do all these jobs faster, better, and safer than ever before in our storied history.

1989.27.119 Whatcom Museum

Seagrave hose & ladder truck "Combination No. 2" stands poised before Fairhaven High School, c. 1913.

1951.22.2 Whatcom Museum

Fairhaven tests its new steam-powered pumper at 12th Street and Harris Avenue, on September 3, 1891. The ornate Fairhaven Hotel, at right, would later be destroyed by fire. While building a bed of hot coals in its boiler, the "steamer" could produce more smoke than the fire it was sent to extinguish. This test also fulfilled a request from the person who donated the steamer, the Honorable Nelson Bennett, who asked to see his gift actually operate before he returned to Tacoma.

1996.10.2387 Biery Collection-Whatcom Museum

The steam-powered Silsby "Bennett" pumper is tested on plank-paved Bay Street near the intersection with Holly Street. The three-horse Combination Wagon #1 stands at the rear. Circa 1907.

1999.60.1 Sandison Collection-Whatcom Museum

Sixteen brass buttons was probably enough rank to put you in charge of a steam-engined pumper drill like this one at Bay and Holly Streets, circa 1907.

Mike Larson Collection

BFD's Continental steam-powered pumper at the waterfront Bloedel Donovan Box Factory and Morrison Mill fire in 1923. This is the "steamer" that was first borrowed, and eventually purchased, from Seattle. The accumulation of ash and cinders on the pier indicates the boiler had been working for quite a while, burning a lot of fuel in the process.

Mike Larson Collection

With "B.F.D." now sculpted into its rear bumper, this ex-Seattle steam-powered pumper was used in October 1924 to fight a large timber blaze near Alger. BFD Chief Frank Stearns (at right) was on scene to command the operation.

1996.10.2412 Biery Collection-Whatcom Museum

Forty years after being replaced by more modern equipment, this restored steam-powered pumper was a hit in a 1953 parade west bound on Holly Street, at the Railroad Avenue intersection. In the hitch of chestnut Belgians, each horse displays a flaxen mane, and a white "blaze" on their face.

1996.57.1 Whatcom Museum

The two-horse Combination (chemical, ladder, and hose) Wagon at BFD's first Station #2 at 12th Street and Donovan Avenue, circa 1910.

Mike Larson Collection

The Bellingham Fire Department, at 12th Street and Donovan Avenue. The driver ("Horseman") is Henry Odell and the dog is "Rex". Hose wagon No. 2 was photographed often, at various locations, and the team of two horses seen here always struck the same pose, with the left horse turned slightly away from the other. The "dappled grey" horses are probably Percheron, a French breed of powerful draft horses that are well fitted to the heavy fire service wagons.

Mike Larson Collection

Hose Wagon No. 2, with the horse team in its favorite, familiar pose.

Tim Marsh Collection

A more docile moment for this three-horse hitch at the Donovan Street Station.

1996.10.2405 Biery Collection-Whatcom Museum

One of a matched pair of brand new chemical wagons paused for inspection on muddy Prospect Street in front of Bellingham's City Hall and jail facility. These wagons were virtually 60-gallon horizontal soda-acid fire extinguishers. When the chemicals were combined, pressure would build and charge the hose which was coiled in the reel on top of the rig.

X.4188.1 *Whatcom Museum*

Three steeds look handsome and ready for action on the wood-plank apron to the original brick, two-bay Station #1/Prospect.

X.4138.1 *Whatcom Museum*

Combination wagon, horse team, and a friendly mutt before the hinged doors of the original Station #1 on Prospect Street. Chief Ben Gibbons (far right) displays a double-breasted uniform with 18 brass buttons, indicating a higher rank than those with only eight or ten buttons.

1996.10.2389 Biery Collection-Whatcom Museum

During BFD's transition from horses to motors, each alarm was a race between those who favored one mode over the other. Chains on the treadless rear tires of the Chief's runabout gave him an advantage in winter, when the horses' hoofs would compact the snow into slippery balls of ice.

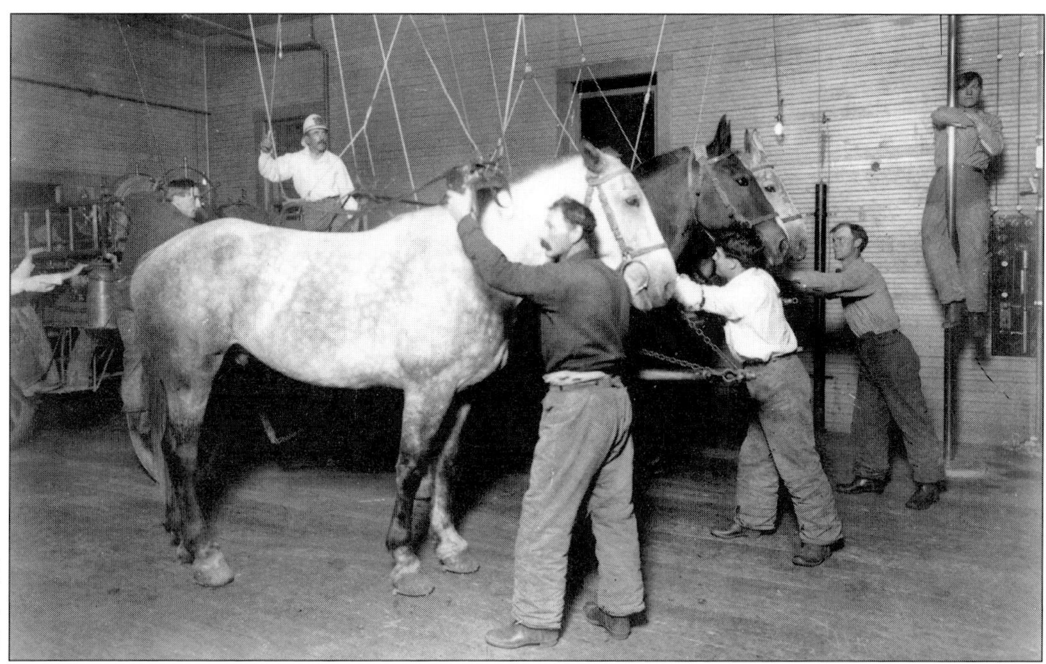

A complicated trapeze lowers the harness system to patient horses, and fire fighters posed for the camera, inside the Prospect Street Station. Heavy wagons required three-horse teams, while lighter weight wagons could get by with two.

1996.10.2378 Biery Collection-Whatcom Museum

1996.10.2374 Biery Collection-Whatcom Museum

Resembling a circus act, men and horses work together at old Station #2 on Donovan Avenue, with their wagon waiting behind. Creatures of habit, the horses were always hitched in the same position within the team.

x.3219.2426a Whatcom Museum

Two dappled roan horses stand alert, ears poised forward, and harnessed to Hose and Ladder Wagon No. 3, along side the original Station #3 at (muddy) Indian and East Maple Streets.

x5024.1 Sandison Collection-Whatcom Museum

If the license plate is any clue, the year was 1923 when this photo was taken of the American La France ladder truck at Station #1 on Prospect. Assistant Chief Ira Cade appears in many BFD photos from that era.

7472 Whatcom Museum

Bedecked with flags and bunting, four vehicles gathered at the old Prospect Street Fire House to join the holiday parade in 1915. BFD's fleet is caught here in a technological transition, with three motorized rigs and one horse-drawn vehicle to ply the brick-paved streets. These three horses were named Dutch, Jack, and Prince.

1968.83.3 Whatcom Museum

A mixture of horse-drawn and motorized rigs gathered at Elk and Magnolia Streets, waiting to join a 1915 parade in honor of the BPOE state convention.

x2676 Whatcom Museum

Flanked by two Seagraves, the high axles of the Chief's Model T "runabout" clear the wooden curbs, as BFD readies its fleet on July 3rd, 1916 for the next day's parade.

Tim Marsh Collection

A young girl bolts from the crowd during a Holly Street parade. Fortunately, she appears to have the undivided attention of the entire crew aboard BFD's Combination No. 1, which leaves a considerable cloud of smoke and dust in its wake.

503 Sandison Collection- Whatcom Museum

The extended length of American La France Ladder Truck #1 often drew the camera's attention. Here the truck rests on Flora Street beside the Gilbert Flats building, which still stands today.

506 Sandison Collection- Whatcom Museum

The American La France Ladder Truck #1 shows its elongated profile again, in front of the ivy-draped rock where the Mount Baker Theater would eventually be built in 1926/27.

502 Sandison Collection- Whatcom Museum

Ladder Truck #1 is poised in front of the original Prospect Station (right) where boilers supplied steam for heat to the adjacent City Hall, through a horizontal iron pipe umbilical. A wood-planked driveway apron connects to the brick-paved street.

506 Sandison Collection- Whatcom Museum

Although no snow drifts are evident, those chains on the smooth, treadless tires of the Chief's Model T helped negotiate the deep muddy ruts of unpaved streets. The Seagrave engine also has chains on its double rear wheels.

505 Sandison Collection- Whatcom Museum

Bricks missing from the façade of the original Prospect Street Station may be evidence of an encounter with one of those new-fangled motor vehicles. From the left: the Chief's convertible roadster; Stutz Engine #3, Stutz Engine #1, a Seagrave combination engine; an American La France ladder truck; a Buick Hose Car.

1989.27.134 Sandison Collection- Whatcom Museum

The variegated brick of the Prospect Street facility, built in 1927, provides background for a quartet of BFD rigs stationed there. From left to right: Engine No.2, Engine No.3, Engine No. 1, and Truck No.1.

Chief Frank E. Stearns appears to be proud of the department's new Dodge roadster staff car, complete with side window curtains, parked along the Boulevard.

x.3219.5346 Sandison Collection-Whatcom Museum

1989.27.161 Whatcom Museum

Preparing to enter the 1925 Tulip Parade, this group mustered in front of the Garden Street United Methodist Church. In 1923, the new Stutz engine cost $13,000, which was $500 cheaper than bids from Seagrave and American La France.

BFD's 1923 Stutz Engine No. 1 shows signs of wear and hard work in this 1938 photo. The rig was finally decommissioned on August 29, 1955.

4189b Sandison Collection-Whatcom Museum

4186 Sandison Collection-Whatcom Museum

With chrome and brass gleaming in the sunlight, American La France Engine #2 (built in 1928) awaits the next call, in front of the hinged, folding doors of the second generation Station #1 on Prospect Street.

1995.1.5840 The Bellingham Herald's Jack Carver Collection – Whatcom Museum

At the shores of Lake Whatcom, Bellingham Fire Dept. Chief Roland Skidmore supervises testing of a new pumper on a brisk January 5, 1949.

"B - F - D" adorns the upper façade of Station #1 on Prospect Street (built in 1927). From the left in this 1937 photo are: the Chief's staff car sedan, the 1930 White "Squad" Engine No. 4, the handsome Stutz Engine No. 1, and the American La France ladder truck. Headlights were sometimes fitted with deep red lenses.

4191 Sandison Collection-Whatcom Museum

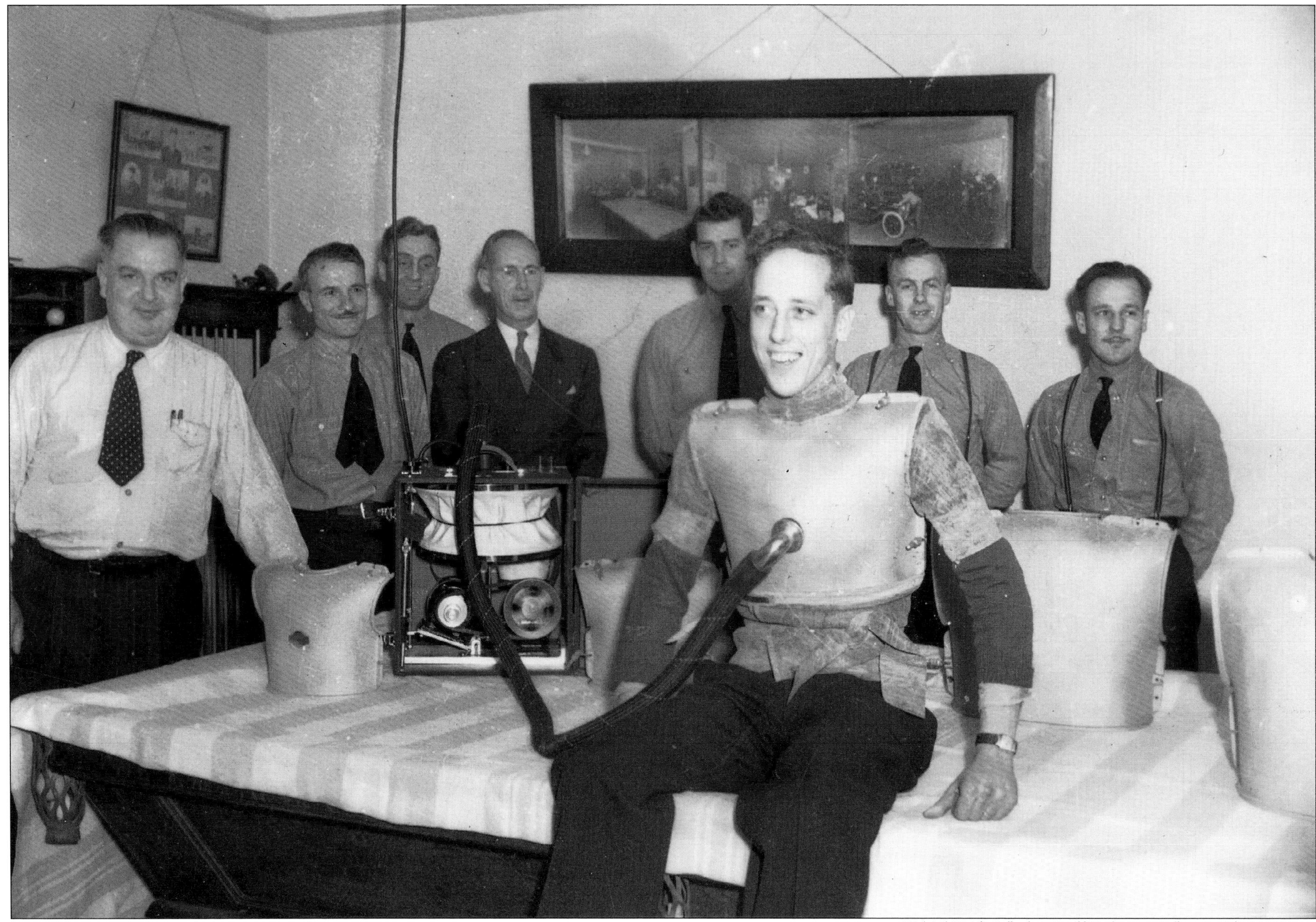

1995.1.5429 The Bellingham Herald's Jack Carver Collection – Whatcom Museum

Fire fighter Art Snow demonstrates the latest in respiration assistance technology, which came to be known as the "lung motor." The device came in three anatomically correct sizes.

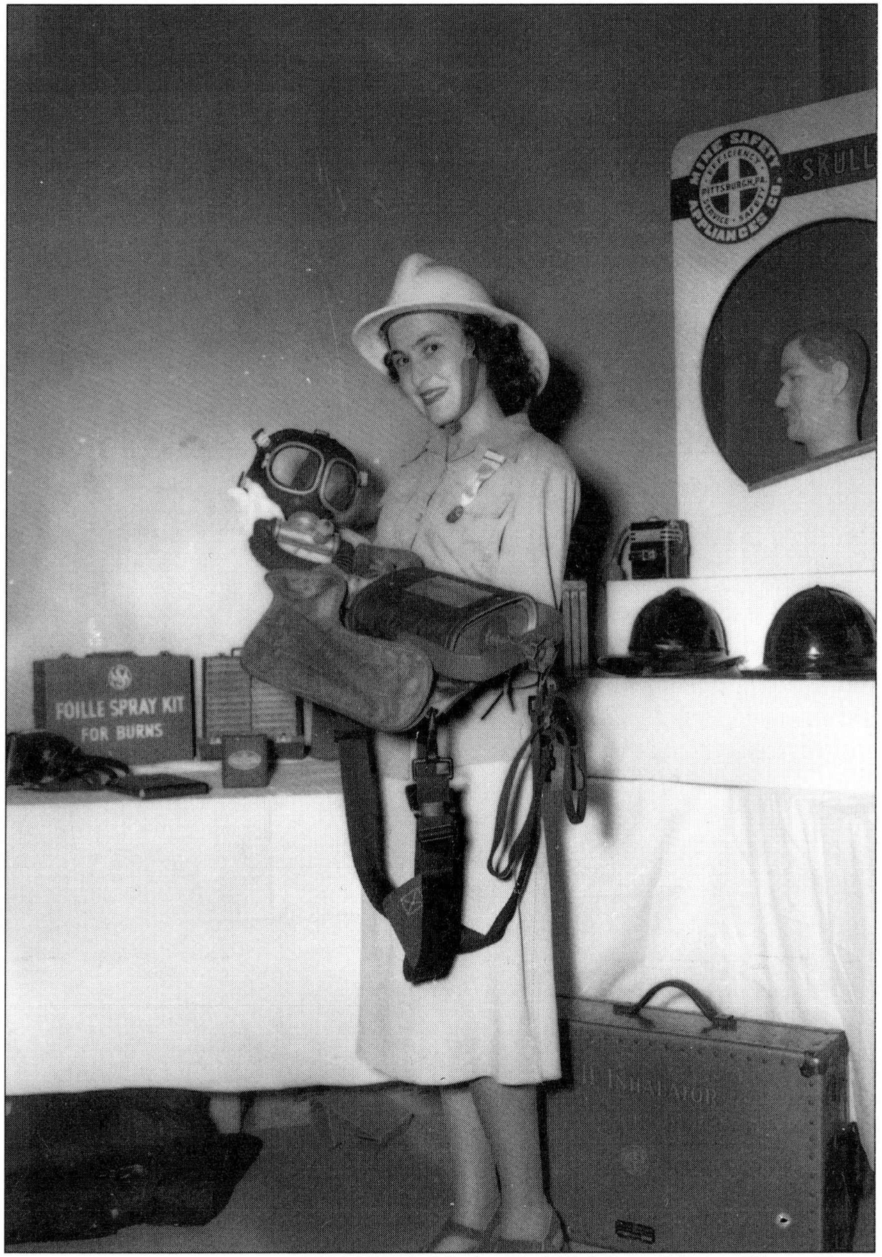

1995.1.3238 The Bellingham Herald's Jack Carver Collection – Whatcom Museum

Ms. Jetta Zoller, from Sumner, shows the latest breathing apparatus technology during the annual convention of the Washington State Fireman's Association, July 29, 1948.

The Bellingham Herald's Jack Carver Collection – Whatcom Museum

Crude equipment by today's standards was all that George Dwelle (left) and Bob Thompson had during response to a fire in the hold of the ship "Galena" at the Pacific American Fisheries dock in Fairhaven, August 11, 1957.

1989.27.143 Whatcom Museum

Seen here in front of City Hall, this 50's vintage Seagrave "Quad" earned its name by providing four fire suppression elements: ladders, hose, water tank, and pump.

1989.27.156 Fred Jukes Studio-Whatcom Museum

The Seagrave "Quad" displays its hose beds and ladder rack.

The Bellingham Herald's Jack Carver Collection – Whatcom Museum

In September of 1970, this American La France aerial ladder rig, a 1965 model, was new to the department. Its gasoline engine may have been the last in a fleet which soon evolved to "all-diesel". After the ladder mechanism was irreparably bent during a collision with Station #3, the entire truck was replaced by a newer (used) diesel, for a cost of $20,000.

1995.14.199 The Bellingham Herald's Jack Carver Collection – Whatcom Museum

A new Crown pumper joined the fleet in March of 1969, with a 500 gallon tank, 1,500 gallons-per-minute pump capacity, and a price of $48,950. It was driven to Bellingham from its assembly plant in Los Angeles by mechanic Bill Brooks and Fire Chief Jack Baker, arriving well after midnight to its dark and quiet new home.

Whatcom Museum

Whatcom Museum

On May 13, 1926 a Stutz engine rolled, spilling its bed full of hose, after failing to negotiate the dreaded "Snake Curves" on Lakeway Drive at Woburn. The vehicle was not insured. Firemen performed repairs and had the rig back in service two days later.

The Bellingham Herald's Jack Carver Collection – Whatcom Museum

On December 20, 1949, this 1930 White "squad" tangled with the bent car still resting in the intersection.

1995.1.5730 The Bellingham Herald's Jack Carver Collection – Whatcom Museum

In this 1949 photograph, the rescue "life-safety net" looks like a pretty small target, even from just a few feet above. Its use proved hazardous to the holders as well as the jumpers. The system was finally abandoned in the late 1970s.

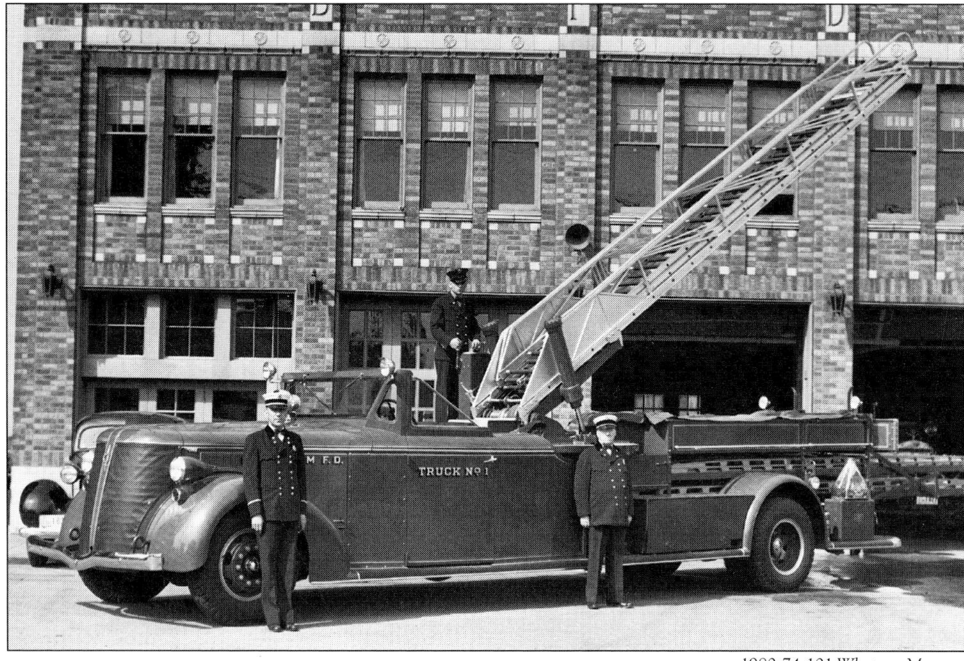

1980.74.101 Whatcom Museum

Ladder Truck No.1 was a 1939 model La France/Foamite, with a 65-foot "reach."

1996.10.510 Biery Collection-Whatcom Museum

Engine #3, a 1981 Van Pelt Pumper, on duty at old Station #3, East Maple and Indian Streets.

1989.27.41 The Bellingham Herald's Jack Carver Collection – Whatcom Museum

The 1963 license plates date this photo, showing two generations of Seagrave pumpers at Station #2, 14th and Harris. The original pair of narrow hinged doors had been replaced by a single overhead door, but it was still a tight fit.

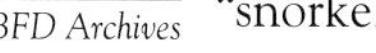

BFD Archives

After years of gallant service, the City's American La France articulated platform "snorkel" was replaced by more modern equipment.

Mike Larson Collection

Western Washington University contributed to the purchase of this Van Pelt aeriel ladder, on the condition that it be kept at Station #3, nearest the campus. It is now "in reserve", replaced by a newer rig with a slightly greater extension. The new aeriel resides at Station #3.

Dave Wolf, BFD Archives

Today's front line aerial is this 1998 Spartan, with a 100-foot L.T.I. aerial ladder and pinable waterway versatility.

x.902 Whatcom Museum

The train came to rest along Railroad Avenue, blocking wood-planked Holly Street, just moments after feuding hoses caused The Great Water Fight, a deep diplomatic embarrassment.

EVENTS

100 Years of Happenings...

The Great Water Fight

By Captain Bob Taylor

Several years before the birth of the Bellingham Fire Department, the independent fire companies serving Whatcom and Sehome demonstrated the go-get'em attitude required of firefighters even today. This fighting spirit revealed itself in spades on June 22, 1891, the day of the inaugural visit of the Canadian Pacific train to our fair community. A gala celebration had been prepared for the Canadian dignitaries aboard the highly anticipated train.

An arch festooned with the U.S. and British flags had been built over Railroad Avenue at Holly Street. Several local patriotic societies waited anxiously to greet the visitors, while two bands stood at the ready to play stirring music.

The uniformed firefighters of Sehome and Whatcom also were on hand, never more in the public eye. The fire companies were positioned on either side of the railroad track not far form the large arch. They each had extended hoselines to prepare a dramatic effect. The rivals would play their hose streams skyward, crossing them in mid-air, creating a sparkling arch as the visiting train drove beneath.

Quite by accident we're sure, one of the fire companies splashed the other as they set up the hoselines. Though their uniforms were dampened their spirits weren't. The offended group returned the gesture. Quicker than a grass fire in August, a furious water fight erupted. The fighting was so fierce that not even a train could make it stop. As it pulled by, the Canadian Pacific was hit with such water force from solid stream nozzles that windows were broken out and the dignitaries on board were drenched.

Center for Pacific NW Studies # 1227

The "Division Street Fire" of 1885 provided both tragic and comic stories. Seventeen buildings were lost, including one that was dynamited to create a fire break. Many volunteers used the rescued liquor to lubricate a "cheer-up meeting" once the fire was out, "...and every motion to adjourn was declared out of order."

The Division Street Fire

By Dave Wolf

(Excerpts taken from The Fourth Corner; History from the Early Northwest, By Lelah Jackson Edson, 1968 edition, Craftsman Press, Seattle)

Chicago had its "great fire" on October 9, 1871.

The massive fire that followed San Francisco's big earthquake on April 18, 1906 did far more damage than the quake.

And, in May of 1885, Bellingham (then the town of Whatcom) had its first conflagration so large that the social and economic impacts would brand the area for decades. Seventeen buildings were destroyed, along with nearly all their contents, for a loss estimated at $35,000 (in 1885 dollars). The event destroyed most of the robust, fledgling business district. A regional economic boom, which eventually peaked in 1889, was already underway, and the commercial district was quickly rebuilt...all along "C" Street, leaving Division Street nothing more than a forgotten alley.

Rumors of arson circulated through the community, and a committee was formed to conduct an investigation, but no formal charges were ever filed. Some accounts said the fire started in the rear of the Steinweg store, while others pointed to the Washington Hotel. Volunteer fire brigades responded, and formed a hand-to-hand bucket line from the bay shoreline. Fortunately, the tide was high.

In her northwest history tome, "The Fourth Corner," Lelah Jackson Edson gives this colorful account:

"Through the night shadowy figures toiled away from the leaping flames from the saloons with bottles and barrels of intoxicants. Gnome-like, they circled their treasure, imbibed deeply, then leaped back to rescue more whiskey."

"After nearly three hours...the Pardon O'Brien building was dynamited ahead of the fire and the flames died for lack of fuel."

Curiously, "...the fire buckets and equipment used so valiantly through the night, all disappeared."

Edson goes on to report that years later, Judge William H. Harris related his memories of the event: *"The fire started in the Washington Hotel early in the night, and before the inmates had gone to bed...The hotel contained the usual bar-room, well stocked with a variety of liquors, and the probable reason why so little of the useful property was saved, was the number who soon energetically worked to save the intoxicants...Many of the fire fighters made frequent trips to the vicinity of the barrels, and after the fire was subdued a 'cheer up' meeting was held there, and every motion to adjourn was declared out of order...Nearly every attendant at the fire had a cup and a cork-screw with him...As the night wore on the meeting dwindled to the last man, who remained in the capacity of watchman."*

B.B. Furniture Fire

By Fire Fighter Beau Whitehead

When an employee of the Martin Electric Company saw flames in the windows of the six-story B.B. Furniture Company building, he quickly turned in the alarm. It was 7:09pm, April 28, 1924. By 7:30pm there were fourteen streams of water pouring onto the building, but the fire raged unchecked. The streams couldn't produce enough pressure to break the windows on the fourth and fifth floors, so policemen shot the glass out with pistols and rifles. Thousands of pounds of hose were carried onto neighboring roofs to fight the fire from above. Gravity-fed hose streams on the ground could only reach as high as the fourth floor and only pressurized streams from the Stutz pumper could reach beyond that.

Had the wind from earlier that day kept blowing, the fire would likely have been uncontrollable, and many more downtown buildings would have been lost.

Volunteer firemen from Everson and the Fire Chief of Mount Vernon arrived to give assistance. The Bellingham Coalmines Company helped out by delivering coal to the steam pumper and Shell Oil brought gasoline to the Stutz.

8,000 people watched the building burn that evening. Five firemen were injured, including some that were cut by shards of falling glass when the bullets shattered the upper windows.

Center for Pacific NW Studies # 523.2

Reported to be the first reinforced concrete building west of the Mississippi, the exterior shell of the BB Furniture Building survived the flames in 1924. Broken upper story windows and the smoke-lapped parapet give evidence of the internal damage. The wood frame Fair Market in the background would eventually fall to fire as well.

1450 Sandison Collection – Whatcom Museum

In this photo, windows were exaggerated by a darkroom technician so they would appear more dramatic when the image appeared in the Herald the next day.

Center for Pacific NW Studies # 522

Sixth floor of the BB Furniture Building after the April 28, 1924 fire. Some 5,500 feet of hose was deployed to provide eight gravity lines and two high pressure lines: one from the Stutz pumper (165 psi, 1300 gpm for two hours) and one from the old steamer (140 psi).

1996.10.557 Biery Collection-Whatcom Museum

Snow and darkness complicated the response to this fire.

Bellingham Manufacturing Fire

By Captain Bob Taylor

Cold weather played a part in many of Bellingham's spectacular fires from the early days. One of these was on January 14, 1947, at the Bellingham Manufacturing plant on Harris Avenue.

A two-story machine shop, this wood framed structure had supplied mechanical parts for the military during World War II. No one knew how the fire started, but flames were shooting through the roof when the alarm was sounded at 9:48 pm. Aided by winds estimated at 75 mph, the fire soon engulfed one end of the Hardwood Fuel building next door. Early firefighting efforts successfully concentrated on saving the exposed building.

Temperatures well below freezing hampered the fire fighting all night. Nozzles that were momentarily shut off froze up and became useless. The reserve engine pump froze while the engine was being moved. Ice formed so thick on the turnouts of the men at the scene that they had to beat each other with spanner wrenches in order to bend their elbows.

When the time came to pick up equipment, the hoses had to be chopped out of beds of the ice on the street. The hoses themselves were solid tubes of ice. They were loaded on long flatbed trucks in sections, and were hauled to the stations to thaw out on the apparatus bay floors. Chief John Bull said this was the most difficult fire in his 27 years on the department.

Photo provided by Clayton Reed

Bellingham played host to the first annual convention of the Washington State Fireman's Association, May 10th and 11th, 1923.

Sandison Collection-Whatcom Museum

About 10:00 am on July 31, 1914, a public trolley collided with BFD's three-horse wagon at East Maple and North Garden Streets. The trolley driver told a reporter he had been "barely moving". The 6,800 pound Chemical and Hose Wagon #3 flipped, injuring three of the five fire fighters who were aboard, but the horses somehow escaped injury.

Diehl Motor Co. Fire

By Captain Bob Taylor

Basement fires are among the most difficult fires to fight. Access is dangerous, air quality is poor, and the threat of building collapse lurks constantly. A spectacular example of these hazards occurred at Diehl Motor Company, at Champion Street and Cornwall Avenue, on December 27, 1948.

Shortly after 2:00 pm, mechanic William Gooding reported smoke coming up a ramp from the basement of the large auto dealership. No one could get through the smoke to see what was burning. Tires, gasoline tanks, and other combustibles were soon involved and burning ferociously.

Bellingham firefighters arrived quickly and tried repeatedly to enter the basement. Equipped with their modern filter masks, they were driven back by smoke too dense for the equipment. Fire Chief Roland Skidmore said, " Our masks require some oxygen in the air to function. Apparently the smoke left no room for oxygen." The Respirator, an oxygen supply vehicle, was put to the test for hours as firefighters overcome by smoke staggered to its location.

As the fire grew, 50 gallon drums of ethyl alcohol antifreeze stored in the basement exploded. Onlookers gaped as the showroom floor collapsed, and one by one new cars slipped into the maw of the now visible roaring fire.

Vast quantities of water were poured into the open basement, and some four hours later the blaze was controlled. Sub-freezing temperatures added to the difficulty of the fight. The firefighters' work continued through the night, as the water that had subdued the fire had to be pumped back out of the basement.

In February, William Gooding was charged with arson in the Diehl Motor fire. He confessed to this crime, and to setting another fire the previous July at a timber company machine shop near the town of Hamilton. Mr. Gooding was 19 years old.

1995.1.3230 The Bellingham Herald's Jack Carver Collection – Whatcom Museum

Two fire fighters were injured combating the blaze in below-freezing temperatures. Some 31 cars were destroyed or damaged.

2003.10.018 The Bellingham Herald's Jack Carver Collection – Whatcom Museum

Diehl Motor Company had been located at Cornwall & Champion for fourteen years. On December 27, 1948 a fire started in the basement and eventually destroyed the building. General manager Robert Diehl estimated the damage to be more than $200,000. "Now we must contemplate building from the ground up," he said. According to the Bellingham Herald, "Fire Chief Roland Skidmore noted that his men were pulling each other out of the building from time to time as one after another weakened and approached helplessness in the smoke." Chief Skidmore was quoted as saying, "Every fireman we had was on the job, including off-shift men. They went in, staggered out, and went in again. It went on and on..."

The Bellingham Herald's Jack Carver Collection – Whatcom Museum

1995.1 The Bellingham Herald's Jack Carver Collection – Whatcom Museum

The Larson Mill burns on the shores of Lake Whatcom, January 16, 1958. The black and white helmet designates the Captain in charge.

Larson Planing Mill

By Captain Bob Taylor

Kiln-dry, highly flammable sawdust filled the air every day at the Larson Planing Mill on Lake Whatcom. In late afternoon on Tuesday, February 13th, 1951, a high-voltage electric short sent workers flying and ignited a spectacular blaze. The flash of fire was followed by a series of others, as electrical contacts set off a chain of exploding short circuits. Mill fireman Si Knott was knocked from his feet by the initial blast. He recovered and sounded an alarm, only to be temporarily blinded and knocked down again in the subsequent explosions.

Plant crews began the firefight with their own equipment, and Bellingham crews rushed to the scene when the alarm bell hit at 5:23. The open structure, the air-stacked lumber, and machinery all fed an inferno of fire stretching throughout the complex. Over 200 gallons of gasoline were consumed by the three fire engines used at the fire.

The mill was a complete loss, along with all its machinery, piles of lumber, and several drying kilns. Other kilns and outbuildings were damaged. Aiding the firefight were a large expanse of asphalt around the buildings and a lack of wind, both of which kept the fire from spreading further.

Photo provided by L.R. Gilfilen

Haagen Anderson snapped this shot of the 1923 Tulip Parade on Cornwall Avenue. The white canopy marks the site where Bellingham High School would later be built.

Center for Pacific NW Studies # 609

The Sehome Apartments, at Berry and Elk (now State) Streets, suffered extensive damage on April 13, 1929. The two upper floors and roof were destroyed, while the lower floor was flooded. In 1929 dollars, the loss was estimated at $30,000.

1995.1.3240 The Bellingham Herald's Jack Carver Collection – Whatcom Museum

As the starter fires his pistol, the Sequim Fire Department tries its hand at the "Make and Break" drill, at Forest and Chestnut Streets, during the Fireman's Convention here on July 29, 1948.

BFD Archives

Sparks from a welder's torch evidently ignited the "overflow oil" in the containment pond around a 10,000-barrel tank at the Puget Sound Pulp and Timber Company. The fire produced lots of black smoke, but little damage.

1995.1.5837 The Bellingham Herald's Jack Carver Collection – Whatcom Museum

Laura Biesheavel's home at 800 Indian Street was gutted by this January 28, 1949 fire.

Fairhaven Hotel Fire

By Fire Fighter Beau Whitehead

Photo provided by E. Rosamonde Ellis Van Miert

On July 27, 1953, the Carousel Club was finishing their dance at the Southside's most celebrated landmark, the Fairhaven Hotel, when the lights in the ballroom flickered. Two men discovered smoke at the electrical junction box, but were unable to stop the fire from spreading into the timbered walls with their extinguishers. Another club member dashed up the hill two blocks to Station #2 to turn in the alarm at 1:56 am. Half an hour had passed since the fire's detection.

Arriving crews knew that the old hotel's dry rafters and foot-thick tar roof would be easy prey for any fire that got a foothold, and an aggressive interior attack was made with four stout handlines. Eyewitness and Fairhaven historian Gordon Tweit gave this account: "Firemen, like devils, began the assault. Danger on all sides; hoses like mammoth snakes writhing." It wasn't long, however, before the ferocious heat forced crews back outside and into defensive operations. The fire was simply too advanced.

The grand hotel burned all night. At dawn, the walls remained standing, but the third floor and roof had been consumed. Four firefighters were injured in the battle, including Pipeman Vern McEwan, whose gloved hand was burned by a red-hot downspout.

The Bellingham Herald's Jack Carver Collection – Whatcom Museum

Embers from the nearby Squalicum Harbor web house fire kept BFD crews busy on the roof of the Georgia Pacific Plywood Company.

The Bellingham Herald's Jack Carver Collection – Whatcom Museum

The Port of Bellingham's "web house" storage facility for the commercial fishing fleet was destroyed January 19, 1954.

Webhouse Fire

By Captain Bob Taylor

A freezing North wind had been blowing all morning on January 19, 1954. Up at old Station #1, future Battalion Chief Marty Morse was so new on the job he hadn't yet worked a fire. It had been a busy day, and Marty was hoping to grab lunch soon. Across the city, at the foot of Mill Avenue, fire had other plans.

At 12:15 pm, smoke was reported in the webhouse owned by the Port of Bellingham. The webhouse was used by fishermen to store their nets and equipment, and contained twenty storage "lockers", all of which were full. In those days, some fishing gear was waterproofed with tar, and barrels of it were kept in these storage areas. As the fire breached the walls and spread into each locker, tar-soaked gear would erupt into flame and explode the barrels nearby. The blast and heat would breach the next wall, and thus the fire marched through the building.

Fierce winds threw brands and embers a hundred yards away, igniting spot fires at the Bellingham Plywood Company. Using their three pumpers and the mill's fire system, fire crews concentrated their efforts there; the webhouse was already lost. The mill-fire was fought by mill-workers, firemen, and twelve water department workers called to the scene by City Water Superintendent Henry Donnelly, who spotted the dark smoke from his Southside home at lunch.

Water froze as it hit the ground on that frosty January day. Firefighter Morse's engine had set up a draft hose from the bay, and Marty remained busy throughout the long shift manning hoselines. At his first fire Marty was wet, cold and still hungry. His initiation as a fireman had begun.

1989.27.152 Whatcom Museum

On November 3, 1977, the city's attention was drawn to a fire at the Antlers Hotel in the Dahlquist Building on State Street. One resident died in the blaze.

Photo provided by Bob Thompson

Working the rear (ally) side of the Dahlquist Building fire.

2003.10.017 The Bellingham Herald's Jack Carver Collection

BFD's aeriel ladder extends into a fourth floor dorm room at WWU's Buchanan Towers, December 16, 1979.

Mike Larson Collection

An on-board explosion scuttled this boat at the Pan American Fisheries dock in Fairhaven. Miles of waterfront require BFD's response to more than just upland structure fires.

1995.1 The Bellingham Herald's Jack Carver Collection – Whatcom Museum

Dousing the embers on June 13, 1975, at the Mt. Baker Plywood mill, 2929 Roeder Avenue.

2003.10.008 The Bellingham Herald's Jack Carver Collection – Whatcom Museum

Four persons were injured in this March 11, 1974 fire at 630 Boulevard, home of a Western Washington State College faculty member.

Center for Pacific NW Studies # 642

The fire which gutted Fairhaven High School (now Fairhaven Middle School) on December 31, 1935, effected the entire community more than most. The displaced students suddenly had to be schooled elsewhere. Split-shift schedules effected parents, businesses, sports, churches...everything. It was, at that time, the oldest high school in the state. The fire was controlled in time to save the new gymnasium from damage.

2003.10.009 The Bellingham Herald's Jack Carver Collection – Whatcom Museum

Possessions were lost, but lives and the structure were saved in this November 1971 fire.

2003.10.010 The Bellingham Herald's Jack Carver Collection – Whatcom Museum

BFD responds to all sorts of automobile mishaps, including this June 12, 1974 event in the 2100 block of Eldridge Avenue.

1996.10.525 Biery Collection-Whatcom Museum

At York and State Streets, the vacant Albers Feed Mill was destroyed in a fire set by transients.

2003.10.016 The Bellingham Herald's Jack Carver Collection – Whatcom Museum

Fire at the Columbia Hotel on State Street, December 31, 1974.

Mike Larson Collection

At 1128 N. State Street, this fire on September 27, 1984 drew cameras from the newspaper across the street. Engine E-53 and Fire Fighter Larson arrived in time to keep the estimated damage at $15,000.

Center for Pacific NW Studies # 1290

Light of the next morning reveals the charred skeleton that somehow held the 700-pound bell in place after this 1962 fire at the City's preeminent icon.

The Bellingham Herald's Jack Carver Collection – Whatcom Museum

On January 14, 1961, this apartment building was reduced to ash, but no one was injured.

Mike Larson Collection

A nighttime blaze consumes the bell tower of the 1892 City Hall.

The Bellingham Herald's Jack Carver Collection – Whatcom Museum

Spectators gather on September 10, 1949, to watch fire fighters attack the flames consuming the Sandwick Building at 11th and Harris Avenue. Today the site is home to "A Lot Of Flowers". The Bellingham Herald reported, "At one point, a damaged 2,300 volt power line, struck by a fire hose, caused the crowd to exercise extra caution."

President
WWU aspirants answer questions
Local, B1

Baseball
NWL, WCL teams to enter tourneys
Sports, D1

Inside
Juvenile jail
Civic Center site favored . . B1
Buddy studies
Getting better grades C1

The Bellingham Herald

May 9, 1988 — A Gannett newspaper — Bellingham, Washington — 35 Cents

Monday

in cyanide trial
nonymous call

workers defy
end strike

ters re-elect
d to 2nd term

Boy rescued from tank

Firefighters, city workers dig 13-month-old free

By DEAN KAHN
of the Herald staff

Tired but happy rescuers broke into applause Sunday night when a 13-month-old boy who fell down a narrow pipe was lifted safely from an unused underground storage tank.

The boy was inside the tank about 2½ hours before being rescued in an effort that began with neighbors offering shovels and ended with the boy cradled in the arms of a physician.

Stephen Ulrich's face was dirty and tear-streaked as paramedics rushed him to an awaiting ambulance for a checkup and a trip to St. Luke's General Hospital. He was treated for a few scrapes and released.

Kim Ulrich

"It was a Mother's Day I won't soon forget," said the boy's mother, Kim Ulrich, 2805 Birchwood Ave.

The boy fell down a foot-wide, 5-foot-long pipe, located a few feet from the side porch of the family home. The fall carried him several more feet onto a pile of dry earth, roots and debris inside the tank, which measured about 6-by-8 feet.

Bellingham firefighter Frank Chorvat spent the several hours of the rescue on his knees, peering down the pipe, listening and calling to the boy, trying to determine if he was all right.

"I did hear him moving," Chorvat said. "When I put his (toy) turtle down (the hole on a rope), he responded" by crawling toward it.

"We knew that he was OK that way," Fire Capt. Ted Loney said.

Kim Ulrich paced and watched from a porch overlooking the rescue effort.

About 15 Bellingham firefighters and seven workers from the Bellingham Public Works Department responded after an emergency call came in about 5:40 p.m.

Neighbors offered shovels, hoses and wheelbarrows to help in the early stages of the rescue, Loney said.

"A lot of people deserve credit," he said.

Don Alderson operated a large city backhoe, digging a hole about eight or nine feet deep next to the tank. Shortly after 7 p.m., wooden siding was dropped into the excavated hole and secured with hydraulic braces to prevent the earth walls from collapsing onto rescuers.

At the same time, a garden hose was dropped down the narrow pipe and air pumped to the boy in the chamber below, just in case earth around the pipe collapsed.

About 7:15 p.m., city Department of Public Works employee Bryan Morse started drilling into the six-inch-thick side of the concrete tank.

Fifteen minutes later, an air-driven jackhammer was lowered into place on a rope and Morse began pounding holes in a circle the size of a rescuer's shoulders.

As Morse drilled, gray dust streamed into his face and drifted above ground. After a 10-minute breather while public works employee Jay Greenwood operated the jackhammer, Morse again took over at 7:42 p.m.

One minute later, he broke through to the interior of the tank. He then started using a smaller, air-powered chipping drill to enlarge the hole.

Paramedic Gerald O'Connor stood nearby, waiting to enter the tank and check on the boy's condition. The boy's white-yellow-and-green Afghan blanket

(Continued on Page A2, col. 4)

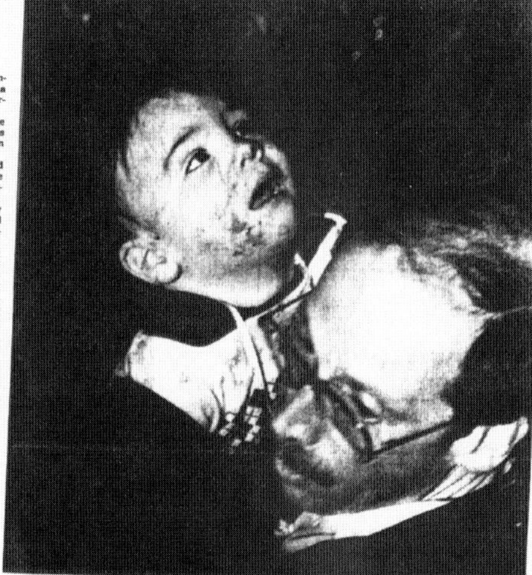

(Herald photos by Pedro Perez)

Stephen Ulrich, 13-month-old son of Kim Ulrich, inset photo at left, is carried to safety by Dr. Marvin Wayne after more than two hours in an underground storage tank.

Graphic: Allen Peterson, Bellingham Herald

Stephen Ulrich was inside the tank for about 2½ hours.

'The little guy just bounced right back'

Less than half a day after Stephen Ulrich was pulled from the shaft of an abandoned cistern, his mother Kim reported that "he's doing real well, like he didn't go through anything at all."

"The little guy just bounced right back."

She praised the work of the rescuers, who retrieved the lad from the chamber in which he spent 2½ hours.

"They did such a good job," she said. "I was impressed how everybody worked together."

The boy's father, Kurt Ulrich, is in Alaska, officials said.

Kim Ulrich said she isn't sure how her son fell down the foot-wide, 5-foot-long concrete pipe.

"It was just one of those things," she said. "I turned my back for a minute and a half. I had the doors shut. By the time I came out, I heard crying.

"I felt so helpless. I think I was more scared than he was."

On May 8, 1988, BFD's Medic One medical director, Dr. Marvyn Wayne, helped rescue a small boy who had fallen into an underground tank.

1995.1 The Bellingham Herald's Jack Carver Collection – Whatcom Museum

On July 31, 1972 this car fell into a "pit" at State and Holly Streets, which was created by an earlier fire that destroyed the Alaska Building.

BFD Archives

Rescue became the issue when a car plunged into the pit at Railroad Avenue and Holly Street, created by the 1994 fire and 1996 demolition of the Mason Building.

Photo provided by Irene Baker

Flames fill the windows of the Alaska Building, on the southwest corner of State and Holly Streets, June 15, 1969. The damage lead to the decision to demolish the building. A bank occupies the site today.

Alaska Building Fire

By Captain Bob Taylor

Sometimes it takes blood to encourage change. At the prominent corner of State and Holly Streets, the Alaska Building burned on June 14th, 1969, taking two lives with it. Started by a resident smoking in bed, the blaze grew to be one of the largest in downtown history. By the time it was done, eight businesses and the landmark building itself were total losses.

Battalion Chief Dave Hewitt arrived after the alarm at 6:37 am with the full complement of BFD on-duty crews: 12 firefighters and four engines. Search crews ran into "a wall of fire" on the second floor, but persevered through worsening heat and smoke, ultimately rescuing nine people. After everyone who could be reached was out of the building, firefighting efforts began in earnest.

By the end, 40 firefighters were on scene, most called from home. The roof and third floor had collapsed, and fire raged unimpeded from the basement to the sky. Two victims were later found in a windowless apartment accessed by an interior hallway.

Chief Wes Baker had recently asked the city council for another fire station, 12 more firefighters to staff it, and 10 additional firefighters to fill out the existing companies. Baker later said the Alaska Building fire could have been controlled much earlier if the department had had the manpower on-duty. Battalion Chief Hewitt agreed: "We had enough men to get the equipment there, but not enough men to fight this kind of fire."

BFD's new Station 5 opened in 1971.

BFD Archives

An early BFD Pontiac ambulance and other rigs take their positions to fight the Alaska Building blaze. Two residents perished in the upper level apartments. Across Holly Street in the distance, the Sunset Building would later suffer a major fire that eventually brought its demolition. At the far right is the Dahlquist Building, where one person died in the Antlers Hotel fire in 1977.

The Uniflite Fire

By Fire Fighter Beau Whitehead

Engine 52 was in quarters watching the NBA finals on April 8, 1980 when they got the alarm. As they pulled out of the station, they could see flames reaching hundreds of feet into the sky from the Uniflite boat plant just eight blocks away. The entire timber-frame structure, some thirty boats, and hundreds of gallons of chemicals, resins, and paint, were engulfed in flames.

Captain Rodenberger arrived on scene and radioed his orders: "F%#k the main building and protect the exposures!" His speedy assessment was right on the money. Nearby stood a tank car filled with resin and several storage tanks containing highly explosive acetones. Railroad crews helped move the tanker and firefighters set up master streams that showered the storage tanks with thousands of gallons of water. The fire in the main building was so intense that crews could only spray the perimeter of the blaze with inadequate handlines. Inside the inferno, fifty-gallon drums of chemicals were exploding regularly.

Station 5's crew, having seen the thermal column from three miles across town, brought the snorkel truck instead of their engine. They took a defensive position and raised two firefighters in its 100' telescoping bucket to operate a high flow nozzle. As the fire intensified, radiant heat began to melt the truck's light bar. In a rush, the outriggers were lifted just enough to drive with the bucket and two firefighters still elevated, causing the entire apparatus to tip back onto its stabilizers. It was a wild ride for the firefighters and a sight long remembered by hundreds of spectators.

Uniflite's vast warehouse and workshop burned well into the next day. The company lost everything. In all, sixty firefighters battled the blaze that spring evening.

Photo provided by Ted Loney

Railroad tank cars were exposed to the heat of the Chris Craft/Uniflite fire deep in the night of April 8, 1980. BFD's aeriel snorkel, at left, fights from above.

Photo provided by Rob Neale

Flames turn the sky bright orange during the Chris Craft/Uniflite fire. Fire Fighter Rob Neale stands atop BFD's aeriel ladder and looks tiny in silhouette against the boiling fury.

Photo provided by Irene Baker

For the 100th Anniversary Fireman's Ball on March 14, 1994, crazed Captain Ken Krumdiack and those unfortunate enough to be placed under his command crafted a detailed, life-size replica of Engine 5. Constructed of wood, foam, and junkyard debris, the ballroom decoration was dismantled immediately after the event at the Lakeway Inn.

Bellingham Pipeline Explosion

By Fire Fighter Brian Wallace

On June 10, 1999, an underground pipeline rupture spilled 229,000 gallons of gasoline into Whatcom Creek. The fuel was ignited in Whatcom Falls Park shortly after 5pm and exploded in a flash that spread one and a half miles down the creek. The blast sent a roiling smoke cloud six miles into the air. Three young boys fell victim to the catastrophe: two ten year-olds who accidentally ignited the spill while playing with fireworks and an 18 year-old who was overcome by the fumes while fishing. Two houses were set aflame in the inferno, and crews from Bellingham, the outlying fire districts, nearby refineries, and the state Department of Natural Resources worked late into the night to douse smoldering fires in the trees and brush along the creek. The damage was devastating, but the fuel had burned up before reaching the more densely populated downtown and waterfront, where countless others could have lost both life and property.

100 YEARS OF COMMUNITY SERVICE
SERVING SINCE
BELLINGHAM
FIRE
DEPT.
1904
1904 - 2004

BFD TODAY

On the Brink of the Next 100 Years...

By Captain Mike Larson

Today's Bellingham Fire Department has changed much since its humble beginnings back in 1904. Six stations, instead of the original two, now provide coverage to a city with a population of 69,800 and an area of 27.8 square miles. One hundred thirty nine uniformed personnel, ten office staff and eleven dispatchers now make up the work force of the department instead of the original twelve members. The Department's apparatus today consists of eight engines, two aerial ladders, a heavy rescue unit, air unit, re-hab unit, arson investigation unit, two haz-mat units, a fire boat, four medic units, six aid units and various command and staff vehicles. The apparatus list in 1904 included just the original single Silsby steam engine, two chemical wagons, one hose wagon, and six hose carts.

Gone are the days of brass poles, street corner alarm boxes, exercising the horses, and playing cards. Fire fighters today must meet state and federal training standards, give tours, conduct fire safety presentations, and maintain facilities and equipment. They perform life safety occupancy inspections, develop occupancy pre-fire plans, review new construction plans to verify code compliance, stay physically fit, and study continuously in order to provide the best service possible.

Today's fire fighters must do all this in lieu of an ever-increasing number of alarms from year to year (there were 12,872 in 2003). Many things have changed since 1904 within the Bellingham Fire Department, but the commitment of its personnel to protect lives and property from the adverse effects of fires, medical emergencies and exposure to hazardous conditions has not changed.

Photo by Martin Kink Jr.

BFD's "A" shift.

Photo by Martin Kink Jr.

BFD's "B" shift

Photo by Martin Kink Jr.

BFD's "C" shift

BFD Archives

"Prospect" dispatcher crew, early 2003.

Photo by Martin Kink Jr.

BFD's administrative personnel

BFD Archives

Engine E-56 joined the fleet in the summer of 2002, to compliment new Station #6. Built by Darley, it cost $450,000, with another $50,000 worth of radios and tools installed after it arrived here. It is the first BFD engine with roll up compartment doors, and the first with Class "A" and "B" foam capacity.

Photo by Jarod Trow

Engine 53 is a twin to Engine 51. Both are 1996 Darleys (with Spartan cabs) rated to pump 1750 gallons per minute at 150 psi.

Photo by Jarod Trow

Rescue 91 is a 1999 Hackney heavy rescue unit equipped to handle the following technical rescue disciplines: trench, confined space, rope, water, and structural collapse.

Photo by Jarod Trow

Ladder 41 is a 1998 Darley, with a Spartan cab, and with a Simon L. T. I. aerial that will support 750 pounds at the tip of its 100' reach. The entire apparatus weighs over 34 tons.

Photo by Jarod Trow

Station #1, built in 1989, is BFD's largest, at 24,658 square feet. A 1999 remodel project created the present Prospect Dispatch Center. BFD's administrative offices are headquartered here.

BFD Archives

Station #3 was remodeled from the ground up in 1984 to accommodate up to eight people and four apparatus. It is the only station that boasts a drive-through bay.

Photo by Jarod Trow

Station #2, occupied in January of 2000, has 8,392 square feet of space and houses up to six persons.

BFD Archives

In 1988, Station #4 relocated from its original location on Alabama Street, to a new facility at 2306 Yew Street, with 8,320 square feet of space.

Photo by Jarod Trow

Station #5 is the smallest, at 4,864 square feet. Built in 1971, the facility was expanded in 1974, remodeled in 1992, and remodeled again in 1994.

BFD Archives

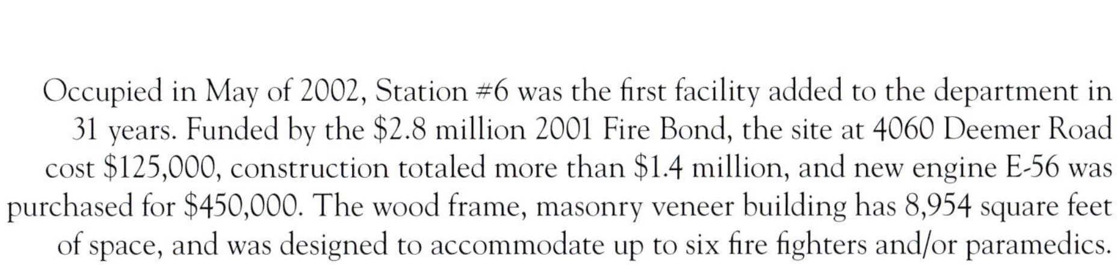

Occupied in May of 2002, Station #6 was the first facility added to the department in 31 years. Funded by the $2.8 million 2001 Fire Bond, the site at 4060 Deemer Road cost $125,000, construction totaled more than $1.4 million, and new engine E-56 was purchased for $450,000. The wood frame, masonry veneer building has 8,954 square feet of space, and was designed to accommodate up to six fire fighters and/or paramedics.

BFD Archives

The Medic One EMS program has two ambulance/paramedic facilities located in the rural county. This crew residence, new in 2003, sits on Grandview Road property owned by Whatcom County Fire District #7.

BFD Archives

BFD's Medic One program purchased and remodeled an existing home at 858 East Smith Road, to serve as a rural county ambulance station, in late 2002.

BFD Archives

BFD's Medic One emergency medical services program currently operates four full-time medic units, with five reserve medic units available when the call load requires additional response capacity. Paramedic bicycle patrols are activated for parades and other large community gatherings.

BFD Archives

Extensive waterfront development requires a water-based response capability. BFD's "Fire Belle" is one of only two identical boats, and was built in Bellingham. She has a twin diesel, twin screw design, with a third diesel dedicated to the water pump. She is as active in rescue work as she is in fire suppression.

BFD Archives

Today's computer-based "Prospect" dispatch center.

ROSTERS

Since it was established in 1904, the Bellingham Fire Department has been the professional home for hundreds of people. Some careers have stretched well beyond 30 years, while others have been brief. Sons have followed in their fathers' footsteps through the ranks. Brothers have worked side-by-side on the fire ground. Despite the inevitable assortment of injuries, BFD has fortunately never suffered an on-duty fatality.

Considerable work has been invested to compile the following historical rosters of BFD personnel. Numerous sources were consulted. Information was checked, and checked again. However, some official records for various periods have disappeared, or perhaps were never maintained in the first place. Every effort has been made to render these rosters as thorough and accurate as possible, within the constraints of the available information.

Fire Chiefs

Name	Start	Finish
Andrew Land	1904	1905
Ben Gibbons	1906	1907
Andrew Land	1908	Died 1909
John J. Marsh	1909	1914
Edwin Hofercamp	1914	1915
John J. Marsh	916	1917
Frank G. Stearns	1/4/1918	1/17/1928
Albert C. (Bert) Sybrant	1/17/1928	1/2/1934
Ira T. Jones	1/2/1934	1/14/1936
S. Everett McGinnis	1/13/1936	6/5/1937
Buford D. Pinkerton	6/5/1937	1/11/1938
Ira T. Jones	1/11/1938	1/12/1942
Buford D. Pinkerton	1/12/1942	3/1/1944
John Bull	3/1/1944	1/5/1948
Roland Skidmore	1/5/1948	6/1/1952
Kennith P. "Joe" Sines, Acting Chief	6/1/1952	7/22/1952
Albert Lyman "Mike" Mohl	7/22/1952	7/17/1956
Wilton Jepperson	7/18/1956	6/16/1958
Wesley Baker	6/17/1958	6/14/1966
Dave Hewitt, Acting Chief	6/14/1966	6/28/1966
Jack Baker	6/28/1966	1978
William "Bill" Bennett, Acting Chief	1978	6/5/1979
Gary Hedberg	6/5/1979	9/15/1984
Jay Gunsauls	12/1/1984	3/19/1999
Mike Leigh	2/10/1999	3/28/2003
William "Bill" Boyd, Acting Chief	3/31/2003	

Uniformed Personnel

Name	ID #	Position	Start	Finish
Andrew Land	*	Chief	1904	1909
Lafe. W Moore	*	Asst. Chief	1904	*
Henry S. Odell	*	Captain	1904	*
Frank D. Alvord	*	Fire Fighter	1904	*
Ora C. Decker	*	Fire Fighter	1904	*
Harry A. Hankins	*	Fire Fighter	1904	*
Charles Bornstein	*	F.F./Callman	1904	*
Will Chandler	*	F.F./Callman	1904	*
Harold A. Martin	*	F.F./Callman	1904	*
Phil D. Tevis	*	F.F./Callman	1904	*
Frank B. Messer	*	F.F./Callman	1904	*
Frank Morris	*	F.F./Callman	1904	*
Myron R. Sorenson	*	Captain	1904	*
Chester I. Camp	*	F.F./Driver	1904	*
John J. Moore	*	F.F./Callman	1904	1905
John D. Thomas	*	F.F./Callman	1904	*
Edmund M. Hansard	*	Captain	1904	*
William Steele	*	Fire Fighter	1905	1905
Ira Cade	*	1st Asst Chief	1905	1932
Frank D. Alvord	*	Fire Fighter	1905	*
Ora C. Decker	*	Fire Fighter	1905	*
Frank B. Jarvis	*	F.F./Callman	1905	*
G. L. Crews	*	Electrician	1905	1918
Tom Warwick	*	Asst. Chief	1905	1932
John J. Marsh	*	Chief	1906	1918
Ben Gibbons	*	Chief	1906	*
William Miles	*	Fire Fighter	*	*
L. Wilson	*	Fire Fighter	*	*
Michael Dwyer	*	Fire Fighter	*	*
Sy Gaffney	*	Fire Fighter	*	*
James L. Odell	*	Fire Fighter	*	*
Joy Holiday	*	Fire Fighter	*	*
Tom Fuller	*	Fire Fighter	*	*
Frank York	*	Captain	*	*
Foster Fay Reed	*	Captain	1907	1912
Albert C. Sybrant	*	Chief	1907	1935
William H. Molzahn	*	Captain	1907	1936
Frank Sterns	*	Chief	1908	1942
Matt Lorang	*	Lieutenant	1910	1918
Ed P. Leonard	*	Lieutenant	1912	1935
W. C. Reed	*	F.F./Driver	1912	1916
Frances J. Leonard	*	Asst. Chief	1913	1944
Edwin Hoffercamp	*	Chief	1914	*
Charles Shepardson	*	Lieutenant	1916	1918
C. E. Riddle	*	*	1917	*
J. M. Riddle	*	*	1917	*
J. M. Arnold	*	*	1917	*
H. Watson	*	*	1917	*
C. F. Restine	*	*	1917	*
F. C. Plantz	*	*	1917	*
J. A. Harkness	*	*	1917	*
W. F. Pancoast	*	*	1917	*
William Sanderson	*	*	1917	*
B. Rollin	*	*	1917	*
F. Fletcher	*	*	1917	*
J. Warwick	*	F.F./Driver	1917	1918
L. B. Brown	*	*	1917	*
G. L. Morgan	*	*	1917	*
L. M. Alexander	*	*	1917	*
Bud Osborne	*	*	1917	*
C. H. Lusby	*	*	1917	*
C. Kramer	*	*	1917	*
Claus Brunlow	*	*	1917	*
John Kastner	*	*	1917	*
E. L. Bardwell	*	*	1917	*
J. A. Sly	*	*	1917	*
W. F. Rohl	*	*	1917	*
W. P. Cummins	*	*	1917	*
Arthur Haight	*	Lieutenant	1917	1928
John Joyce	*	Fire Fighter	1917	1918
John Bakke	*	Fire Fighter	1918	1918
E. C. Darrin	*	*	1918	1918
Forrest A. Fuller	*	Operator	1918	1942
Buford D. Pinkerton	*	Chief	1918	1944
Elmer C. Park	*	Fire Fighter	1918	1941
Herbert Miller	*	Electrician	1918	1920
William Loveland	*	Fire Fighter	1918	1918
E. Duval	*	Fire Fighter	1918	1918
Edward Haight	*	F.F./Driver	1918	1921
Alford Brewer	*	Fire Fighter	1918	1918
Otto W. Johnston	*	Fire Fighter	1918	1918
Jack Park	*	Fire Fighter	1918	1918
Charles Neff	*	Fire Fighter	1918	1919
W. H. Phillips	*	F.F./Driver	1918	1919-
Ernest Ahlman	*	F.F./Driver	1918	1920
Clarence Nichols	*	F.F./Driver	1918	1921
Ernie Cassils	*	Captain	1918	1942
H. Carl Dorr	*	Fire Fighter	1918	1919
R. Armstrong	*	Fire Fighter	1918	1918
Leo Gordon	*	F.F./Driver	1918	1923
Frank Smith	*	Fire Fighter	1918	*
Paul Smith	*	Fire Fighter	1918	1920
William Crabill	*	Fire Fighter	1918	1919
Sanford E. McGinnis	*	Chief	1918	1942
Ira T. Jones	*	Chief	1919	1943
Ed Peterson	*	Asst. Chief	1919	1945
Vernon Smith	*	Fire Fighter	1919	1946
George Lockhead	*	Fire Fighter	1919	1923
Harry F. Parker	*	Captain	1919	1944
William Smith	*	Fire Fighter	1919	1920
Lee A. Park	*	F.F./Driver	1919	1945
Elmore Moore	*	Fire Fighter	1920	1944
Halbert W. Lyle	*	Fire Fighter	1920	1947
Lyle Halbert	*	Captain	1920	1947
Floyd M. Nickerson	*	Captain	1920	1945
John E. Bull	*	Chief	1920	1948
Roy J. Johnson	*	Fire Fighter	1920	1921
Milliard F. Stoddard	*	Captain	1921	1938
Harry S. Jenkins	*	Alarm Sup/Elec	1921	1945
Ernest A. Koger	*	Asst. Chief	1921	1948
George W. Sterns	*	Fire Fighter	1923	1948
LeRoy Sturgis	*	Captain	1923	1951
Harvey S. Pinkerton	*	Inspector	1924	1947
Robert R. Renahan	*	Mechanic	1925	1927
Clarence H. Dean	*	Capt.Chief Sec	1925	1948
James B. Johnson	*	Fire Fighter	1925	1949
Lyle Nugent	*	Fire Fighter	1925	1926
Ray R. Moblo	*	Fire Fighter	1925	1947
Percy W. Moblo	*	Fire Fighter	1926	1943
Rueben E. Jones	*	Captain	1926	1948
Milliard F. Nunley	*	Dispatcher	1926	1950
Sam P. Rust	*	Asst. Chief	1926	1951
Bert W. Groom	*	Battalion Chief	1926	1952
William Ball	*	Fire Fighter	1927	1941
Roland J. Skidmore	*	Chief	1927	1952
William Y. Evans	*	Asst. Chief	1927	1952
William D. Clifton	*	Mechanic	1927	1942
George M Zeigler	*	Fire Fighter	1927	1928

Name	ID #	Position	Start	Finish
James Gibbons	*	Fire Fighter	1928	1928
Al F. Anderson	*	Chief Inspector	1928	1946
Donald Ball	*	Fire Fighter	1928	1949
Martin Jensen	*	Fire Fighter	1928	1939
Charles E. Messick	*	Fire Fighter	1928	1957
Roy G. Pike	*	Fire Fighter	1928	1945
Albert L. Mohl	*	Chief	1928	1958
Mark B. Cooper	*	Captain	1928	1954
Frank Corey	*	Fire Fighter	1930	1944
Kenneth Sines	*	Asst. Chief	1930	1957
F. M. Nickerson	*	*	1934	1944
Roland Thomas	*	*	1936	1939
Joe Schlanger	*	*	1936	1941
Dennis Dobson	*	*	1937	1941
Ralph Hennes	*	Captain	1938	1954
James B. Watkins	*	Captain	1938	1963
Irv L. Knutsen	*	Battalion Chief	1938	1966
MacRae Stone	*	Asst. Chief	1939	1966
Wilt Jepperson	*	Chief	1939	1969
Frank Day	*	Captain	1942	1967
Gene Sybrant	*	Captain/Sec.	1942	1960
William Bronsema	*	Mechanic	1942	1953
Alton Jepperson	*	Captain	1942	1968
Fred B. Barmore	*	Fire Fighter	1942	1946
Hugh Wager	*	Fire Fighter	1942	1945
Edward Lund	*	Fire Fighter	1942	1952
Wesley Baker	*	Chief	1942	1966
Victor M. Bundy	*	Asst. Chief	1942	1966
G. S. Bonner	*	*	1944	*
Zane F. Hickok	*	*	1944	*
C. E. Barnhart	*	Fire Fighter	1944	*
Wilber Bundy	*	Fire Fighter	1944	*
E. O. Meador	*	Fire Fighter	1944	1945
R. E. Shell	*	*	1944	*
L. Jensen	*	Fire Fighter	1944	1945
J. B. Johnson	*	Fire Fighter	1944	*
Donald Edwards	*	Fire Fighter	1945	1946
Robert H. Moblo	*	Asst. Chief	1945	1976
DeWitt D. Dunhaver	*	B.C. Signals	1946	1968
Ben W. Henkle	*	Captain	1946	1975
David L. Hewitt	*	Acting Chief	1946	1971
Arthur B. Snow	*	Battalion Chief	1946	1972
Jack Gaskill	*	Fire Fighter	1946	1962
Walter G. Phillips	*	Fire Fighter	1946	1969
Alfred Barnes	*	Asst Electrican	1946	1970
Kenneth Peterson	*	Fire Fighter	1946	1946
Herbert L. Murray	*	Fire Fighter	1946	1947
Lawrence Ashton	*	Fire Fighter	1946	1946
Flores W. Weaver	*	Fire Fighter	1946	1970
Cecil Urquhart	*	Captain	1946	1971
James Keeler	*	Fire Fighter	1946	1947
Adrian Fuller	*	Fire Fighter	1947	1948
John W. Dries	*	Fire Fighter	1947	1953
Harold C. Kolb	*	Captain	1947	1975
Winfred Ira	*	Fire Fighter	1947	1966
Wesley Smith	*	Fire Fighter	1947	1948
Eugene B. Hershey	*	Captain	1948	1974
Kenneth C. Rollag	*	Fire Fifgter	1948	1951
Gene A. Long	*	Captain	1948	1972
Jack Baker	*	Chief	1948	1978
Kenneth H. Reimers	*	Captain	1948	1978
Alvin Boe	*	Battalion Chief	1948	1972
Clayton F. Reed	*	Battalion Chief	1948	1972
Ronald Buell	*	Fire Fighter	1948	1965
Donald Pilkey	*	Fire Fighter	1948	1950
Francis Monks	*	Fire Fighter	1949	1953
Donald Goodell	*	Fire Fighter	1950	1951
Clyde Sines	*	Battalion Chief	1950	1978
Lawrence D. Miller	*	Captain	1950	1975
Robert Baunach	*	Battalion Chief	1950	1976
Kenneth Smith	*	Battalion Chief	1950	1977
Don W. Smith	*	Fire Fighter	1950	1978
Vernon McEwen	*	Captain	1951	1974
Walter Johnson	*	Dispatcher	1951	1974
Thomas Rawls	*	Fire Fighter	1951	1954
Robert Thompson	*	Captain	1951	1977
Elmer G. Woodell	*	F.F./Driver	1951	1974
George Bennett	*	Acting Chief	1951	1979
Arthur Hendrickson	*	Captain	1952	1979
Ole Olson	*	Battalion Chief	1952	1983
Harold E. Byers	101	Captain	1952	1979
Peter Sabastian	*	F.F./Driver	1952	1967
Ralph Gilfilen	*	Captain	1952	1979
Lyle Kuhns	*	Captain	1952	1977
Richard Payne	*	F.F./Driver	1952	1977
George M. Johnson	*	F.F/Driver	1952	1977
Frank E. Black	*	Captain	1953	1978
George Wisbey	*	Inepector	1954	1980
Martin Morse	102	Battalion Chief	1955	1984
Frank Meyer	103	Captain	1955	1978
George Dwelle	*	Fire Marshal	1955	1969
Robert Kuhns	*	Captain	1955	1981
James Palmer	104	Dispatcher	1955	1983
Gil Soderquist	105	Captain	1955	1976
James Mortimer	*	Captain	1957	1985
Billy Frey	*	F.F./Driver	1957	1979
Delbert Sturgis	106	Inspector	1958	1991
Delbert Jones	107	Battalion Chief	1961	1982
Dan Early	108	Dispatcher	1962	1985
Charles Tuttle	109	F.F./Driver	1963	1992
John D. Lanford	110	Fire Marshal	1964	1982
Leo Nielson	111	Dispatcher	1966	1984
Gary Hedberg	112	Chief	1966	1998
Alan Drafs	113	F.F./Driver	1966	1997
Don Wright	114	Captain	1966	1991
Don Spady	115	Battalion Chief	1966	1984
Dana Nichols	116	F.F./Driver	1966	1989
Jim Holding	117	Fire Fighter	1965	1972
Doug Reid	118	Captain	1967	1997
Robert Spady	119	F.F./Driver	1967	1988
Ted Loney	120	Captain	1967	1998
Steve McIvor	121	F.F./Driver	1967	1997
Jim Bliven	122	Captain	1968	1989
Lee Binschus	123	Inspector	1968	1984
Robert Marsh	124	Captain	1968	1995
Frank Chorvat	125	F.F./Driver	1968	1997
Larry Raethke	126	Captain	1968	1993
Harold Miller	127	F.F./Driver	1968	2001
Bob Lovelace	128	M.S.O.	1969	1996
Harry Rodenberger	129	Battalion Chief	1969	1997
Fred Kunzmann	130	Captain	1969	1987
Larry Moore	131	Paramedic	1970	
Alan Hershey	132	F.F./Driver	1970	2002
Norm Chamberlain	*	Inspector	1971	1977
Chuck Dawson	*	Fire Fighter	1971	1979
Hartwell Mitchell	133	Sr. Inspector	1971	1999
Gary Schemstad	134	F.F./Driver	1971	1993
Ron Delcamp	135	Captain	1971	1988
Larry LaBree	136	Battalion Chief	1971	
Mike Willson	137	F.F./Driver	1971	
James White	138	Captain	1971	
Fred Urquhart	139	Captain	1971	2002
Jim Yake	140	Paramedic	1971	2000
John Kunnap	141	Captain	1971	
Jim Kolb	142	Sr. Inspector	1971	2003
Jerry Shearer	143	Paramedic	1971	2001
Ron Morehouse	144	Battalion Chief	1971	
Robert Peterson	145	Battalion Chief	1972	
Tom Hillman	*	Fire Fighter	1972	1973
Rick Eherenfieldt	146	F.F./Driver	1972	1999
Don Beattie	147	Battalion Chief	1972	
David Ceranova	148	F.F./Driver	1972	
Mike Meyer	149	Paramedic	1973	1987
Mike Leigh	*	Chief	1973	2003
Warren D. Pauley	150	Asst. Dispatcher	1973	
Stuart R. Johnson	*	Fire Fighter	1973	1974
Gerry Williamson	*	Paramedic	1974	1978
Danny Anderson	151	Captain	1974	
Roger Iverson	152	F.F./Driver	1974	2002
Chuck Dederick	153	Battalion Chief	1974	
Glenn Oltman	154	F.F./Driver	1974	
Dan Ohms	155	Q.A.C.	1974	
Dale Long	156	F.F./Driver	1974	
Siegfried Snapp	157	Div. Chief	1974	1997
Gary Nichols	158	Fire Fighter	1974	1996
Doug Marsh	159	Captain	1974	
Dan Benckendorf	160	F.F./Driver	1974	
Bryan McDonald	161	Captain	1974	
Glenn Pauley	162	Paramedic	1974	2001
David Hammers	163	M.S.O.	1974	
James T. Smith	164	F.F./Driver	1974	
Ron Gustafson	165	Paramedic	1974	1982
Jerry Bailey	166	Captain	1974	
Rick Ambrose	167	F.F./Driver	1974	
Alan Martin	168	Captain	1974	

Name	ID #	Position	Start	Finish
William Pudell	169	Captain	1975	
Ken Krumdiack	170	Captain	1975	
John Bartleson	171	Paramedic	1975	1998
Brian A. Hahnel	*	Fire Fighter	1975	1976
Brian Caven	172	Paramedic	1977	1998
Floyd Roorda	173	Captain	1977	
Rick Leamer	174	Fire Fighter	1977	1985
Kim Hurlbut	175	Captain	1977	
Kreig McBride	176	Captain	1978	
Jim Burton	177	Fire Fighter	1978	2000
Neil Carlberg	178	F.F./Driver	1978	
Kurt Duey	179	F.F./Driver	1978	
Roger Brock	180	F.F./Driver	1978	
John Lowry	181	Fire Fighter	1978	1990
Don Davis	182	Paramedic	1978	1982
Gerald O'Connor	183	Captain	1979	
Rob Neale	184	Fire Marshall	1979	1995
Jeff Jaquish	185	Captain	1979	
Dave Tveit	186	Paramedic	1979	
Steve Lamoureaux	187	Battalion Chief	1979	
Dan Douge	188	Paramedic	1979	
Ken Gustafson	189	Div. Chief	1979	
Graydon Bundy	190	F.F./Driver	1979	
Don Paton	191	Paramedic	1980	
Pete Sallee	192	Captain	1981	
Mike Larson	193	Captain	1981	
Donald L. Smith	194	Sr. Inspector	1982	
Keith McLean	195	F.F./Driver	1982	
David Fayram	196	Probationer	1982	1983
Don Davis	197	Inspector	1983	
Martin Kink	198	F.F./Driver	1983	
Doug Shaffer	199	Fire Fighter	1983	2000
Michael Hurlbut	200	F.F./Driver	1983	
Brad Bannerman	201	Captain	1983	
William Boyd	202	Chief	1983	
Marv Streubel	203	Paramedic	1984	
Cary Gustafson	204	Captain	1984	
Jay Gunsauls	205	Chief	1984	1999
Robert Wilson	206	Paramedic	1985	
James Morell	207	Paramedic	1985	
Andy Day	208	Captain	1985	
Kahni Tuson	209	F.F./Driver	1985	
Jerry Stougard	210	F.F./Driver	1985	
Greg Bass	211	Paramedic	1985	2001
Antony McGuinn	212	Paramedic	1987	
Jim Lane	213	Paramedic	1987	
Mark Hill	214	Probationer	1988	1988
Craig Bruner	215	F.F./Driver	1988	
Brian Flannelly	216	Paramedic	1988	
Jim Peeples	217	Fire Fighter	1988	
Chuck Henkel	218	Captain	1988	
Mark Tarabochia	219	F.F./Driver	1988	
Robert L. Gray	220	Captain	1988	
Joseph Bertels	221	Paramedic	1988	
Wendy Paton (Cargile)	222	Paramedic	1989	2000
John Scurlock	223	Paramedic	1989	
Roger Christensen	224	Paramedic	1989	
Robert Taylor	225	Captain	1990	
Tanya Pierce	226	Probationer	1990	1990
Steve James	227	Paramedic	1990	
Scott Farlow	228	Paramedic	1990	
Jay Comfort	229	Captain	1990	
Kenny White	230	Paramedic	1990	
Randy VanderHeiden	231	Paramedic	1990	
Jerry Martin	232	Paramedic	1990	
Keith Moberg	233	Probationer	1990	1991
Jim Spear	234	Fire Fighter	1991	1993
Gordon Neitling	235	Paramedic	1991	
Rob Stevenson	236	Medic Capt.	1991	
Scott Peterson	237	Fire Fighter	1992	
Greg Sluys	238	Inspector	1992	
Pam Turner	239	Paramedic	1992	
Denice Jones	240	Probationer	1993	1993
Bob Coston	241	Fire Fighter	1994	
Erica Martin	242	Paramedic	1994	
Tim Kays	243	Fire Fighter	1995	
Mannix McDonnell	244	Paramedic	1996	
Joe Gahms	245	Probationer	1996	1997
Shelly Brown (Lipscomb)	246	Probationer	1996	1996
Todd Nordmeyer	247	Fire Fighter	1996	
Michael Ray	248	Fire Fighter	1996	
Ryan Provencher	249	Paramedic	1996	
Brody Loy	250	Fire Fighter	1996	
Rich Kittinger	251	Paramedic	1997	
Sean Farnand	252	Paramedic	1997	
Bill Stockley	253	Fire Fighter	1997	2001
Jon Denham	254	Fire Fighter	1997	
Mike Hammes	255	Fire Fighter	1997	2000
Jason Garat	256	Paramedic	1997	
Dave Parker	257	Fire Fighter	1998	
Marie Bussard	258	Paramedic	1998	
Devon Pelkie	259	Paramedic	1998	
Kelly Devlin	260	Paramedic	1998	
Kurt Bruland	261	Paramedic	1998	
Kurt Jensen	262	Fire Fighter	1998	
Colin Lowin	263	Fire Fighter	1998	
Dave Stephan	264	Fire Fighter	1998	
Phil Puhek	265	Paramedic	1998	
Shawn Linville	266	Med. Student	1998	
Andrew Trimakas	267	Paramedic	1998	
Scott Hall	268	Paramedic	1998	
Jeff Brubaker	269	Paramedic	1998	
Jason Karwhite	270	Fire Fighter	1998	
Mike Leigh	271	Chief	1999	2003
J. Scott Hansen	272	Fire Fighter	1999	
Jeff Sallaway	273	Fire Fighter	1999	
Dave Pethick	274	Paramedic	1999	
Warren Scotter	275	Fire Fighter	1999	
Brian Jones	276	Fire Fighter	1999	
Eric Kirkpatrick	277	Fire Fighter	1999	
Jason Sims	278	Fire Fighter	1999	
Kelly Gambini	279	Fire Fighter	1999	
Darren Wood	280	Paramedic	1999	
Ron Richard	281	Fire Fighter	2000	
Todd Lagestee	282	Fire Fighter	2000	
Corry Morris	283	Fire Fighter	2000	
Bryant Walvatne	284	Fire Fighter	2000	
Julian Lindsay	285	Paramedic	2000	
Tobey Stevenson	286	Fire Fighter	2001	
Beau Whitehead	287	Fire Fighter	2001	
Willie Spaulding	288	Med. Student	2001	
Dan McDermott	289	Fire Fighter	2001	
Chris Starkey	290	Fire Fighter	2001	
Denice Dierich	291	Med. Student	2001	
Jeff Reinke	292	Fire Fighter	2001	
Brian Cain	293	Fire Fighter	2001	
Ray Young	294	Fire Fighter	2001	
Todd Fisher	295	Fire Fighter	2001	
Eric Postma	296	Fire Fighter	2002	
Scott Farrell	297	Med. Student	2002	
Matt Fleming	298	Med. Student	2002	
Christian Carson	299	Fire Fighter	2002	
Matt Davis	300	Fire Fighter	2002	
Jeff Onzay	301	Fire Fighter	2002	
Shawn Haynes	302	Fire Fighter	2002	
Dan Robertson	303	Probationer	2002	2002
Johnathan Huntley	304	Probationer	2002	2002
Joe Linn	305	Probationer	2002	2002
Jarod Trow	306	Fire Fighter	2003	
Ed Jirsa	307	Fire Fighter	2003	
Brian Wallace	308	Fire Fighter	2003	
Cole Younger	309	Fire Fighter	2003	
Ryan Gilbert	310	Fire Fighter	2003	

* Information Not Available

Administrative Personnel

Name	Start	Finish	Name	Start	Finish
Marian Boe	1962	1993	Kim Keck	1994	1995
Dr. Marvin Wayne	1974		Karin Artmann	1995	1996
Debra Peterson	1975		Laura Richardson	1993	1996
Linda Almen	1978	1986	Paula Rickenbacker	1999	2001
Lora McMurry	1983		Janice Wilson	1996	
Jann Bruland	1986	2003	Shelley Muzzy	1996	
Fern Shaffer	1989		Dave Wolf	1997	2003
Shonda Williams	1991	1992	Mayrus Helberg	2001	
Sandy Howard	1992	1993	Joyce Anderson	2001	
Jill Cratsenberg	1993	1993	Faith Foster	2004	

"Prospect" Dispatch Personnel

Name	Start	Finish	Name	Start	Finish
Anita Parks	1999		Kent Poortinga	1999	1999
Gayle Peeples	1999		Faith Foster	1999	2003
Angie Ratayczak	1999		Traci Lester	1999	
Cindy Sluys	1999		Steve Kerzman	2001	2003
Toni Carpenter	1999		Micah Quintrall	2002	
Stacy Tillsley	1999		Susan Hanson	2003	
Sheila Hanlon	1999		Clint Herman	2004	
Debbie Bailey	1999	2000			

BUSINESS PARTNERS

Louis Auto Glass Celebrates 75th Birthday

Louis Auto Glass celebrates its 75th year serving Northwest Washington in 2004. The company is currently in its fourth generation of continuous family ownership and operation.

Despite the many changes in car styles and auto glass installation methods since 1929, the company, owned by the Adelstein family, has never faltered in its commitment to its customers and the local community.

"My grandfather, Louis Adelstein started the company in 1929 selling auto parts, accessories and installing auto glass," says Rick Adelstein, president and current owner. As the country emerged from the Depression, the company needed a bigger building. That led in 1941 to construction of the current Louis Auto Glass main store in Bellingham on North State Street. At the time, the location was far outside the main commercial district of Bellingham.

Our Bellingham store has served the company since 1941.

"People thought he was crazy to build there," says Mel Adelstein, Louis' son. "But, Bellingham just kept growing. Before long we were in the middle of town. My dad was also committed to giving his customers the best, so they didn't seem to mind that our location was out of the way."

That building has served as the Bellingham store and main headquarters for 63 years and from here the family has directed the company's growth. Expansion took hold in 1987 when a branch was established in Lynden and in 1990 when the company expanded to Mt. Vernon.

Both Lynden and Mt. Vernon were natural steps in the company's growth, says President Rick Adelstein. We knew that customers liked our quality and how we took care of them. We believed that customers in other nearby cities would appreciate that. By staying close, we are able to keep our high standards. "Our active marketplace now runs from the Canadian border to Everett," says Adelstein. "But the heart of our company still beats in Whatcom and Skagit counties.

Second-generation owner Mel Adelstein stays active in the company. He stands next to the company's 1929 Ford Model A.

Louis Auto Glass is proud to be supporting our communities. Our customers have given us their trust and support for 75 years so donating back to the community is our way of saying thanks. Some of the organizations supported by Louis Auto Glass include:

March of Dimes; Mt. Baker Theater; Whatcom County Museum; Western Washington University Athletics; President's Club - Western Washington University; American Red Cross; Arthritis Foundation; Big Brothers/Big Sisters; Boys and Girls Clubs; United Way; American Cancer Society; American Diabetes Association; Whatcom Police Association; Various Sports Teams and Events; Bellingham Chamber of Commerce; Mt. Vernon Chamber of Commerce; All Local Schools; Lion's Clubs.

BUILDERS ALLIANCE

Thank you Bellingham for your support over the past 90 years!

Builders Alliance has come a long way since its inception in 1913 as Bellingham Sash & Door. Just as Bellingham and its surrounding communities have grown and evolved, so have we. Through all the changes, one thing has remained constant - we continue to be a local, family owned company, focused on serving our community. What we are especially proud of, though, is that we have been able to be part of the history of this wonderful community we live in, and for this we thank you, our customers.

In the beginning, Bellingham Sash & Door primarily operated as a sawmill and manufactured doors, windows and trim. After Bellingham Sash & Door opened its store at 600 West Holly Street, the focus began to change. In 1960, the current owners purchased the company and then began the change from manufacturing to distribution and sales of building materials. As Bellingham grew, so did the business. In 1993, we opened our current location opened at 3801 Hannegan Road, which has allowed us to continue to grow and better serve you.

Today, Builders Alliance still holds high the core values of having a quality, customer service oriented staff whose focus is to help you successfully complete your project, big or small.

Thank you again for being part of our first 90 years, and for allowing us to be part of the history - and future - of Bellingham!

CASCADE LAUNDRY

205 Prospect • Bellingham • 734-4200

Back in the late 1800's, Cascade Laundry pioneered the laundry cleaning business in the Whatcom County area. Since then, we have set and continued a pace of progress and growth that has left a favorable impression on our clients. We have come a long way since our horse drawn laundry wagon first clattered down old Dock Street (now Cornwall Avenue).

For over 100 years, we have provided a service that meets the needs of our community. Our existence today exemplifies our ability to meet the constant challenges and demands placed upon our business through the years.

We are proud to be Bellingham's oldest and most progressive, locally owned laundry business, and we will continue to meet the challenges of tomorrow.

Cascade Laundry and Cleaners Inc. 1926

Remembering our Past

In May 1939, the City of Bellingham Employee's Credit Union was incorporated.

In 1982 we became Public Employees Credit Union.

The Bellingham Fire Department circa 1930; now the Syre Educational Center, served as our first branch *

Celebrating our Future

In 1998 to incorporate our community charter, the name was changed to North Coast Credit Union.

North Coast now serves over 17,000 members. Wow! We still provide free checking, free online banking, low fees, free smiles and excellent service.

Call 733-3982

NCUA

* Photo courtesy of Whatcom Museum of History & Art.

You can be a member. Experience the North Coast Difference today!

OVERHEAD DOOR®

the original since 1921

Overhead Door — 202 Ohio St., Bellingham

Doors on Bellingham Fire Station #6 — 2003

Overhead Door Corporation pioneered the garage door and opener industry producing the first upward-lifting garage door in 1921 and the first electric door opener in 1926. Overhead Door has over 400 independent distributors throughout the United States and Canada.

Larry Erickson opened the locally owned Overhead Door Company of Bellingham in 1956. He then sold it to his long time employee, Del Gilliam in 1978 who worked closely with his two sons, Terry and Gary, finally turning it over to them in 1992. Del Gilliam's son-in-law, Jack D. Johnson started with the company in 1980 and purchased the family business in 1998.

For almost 50 years our company has prided itself with providing quality residential, commercial and industrial products, along with fast professional service to all of our customers.

All of us at Overhead Door thank the City of Bellingham Fire Department for entrusting us to keep your Overhead Doors working properly, enabling you to respond quickly in a time of emergency. It's been our privilege to serve the community in this way and we hope to for the next 100 years.

Follis Realtors

William T. Follis Sr. – Founder

William T. Follis Jr.

W. Thomas Follis

Founded by Wm. T. Follis Sr. in 1921 and serving Bellingham and Whatcom County from offices always located in the downtown Bellingham area, Wm. T. Follis, Realtors is Bellingham's oldest, independent real estate company.

His son, Wm. T. Follis Jr., joined the firm in 1946, beginning the Appraisal Division. In 1970, his grandson, W. Thomas Follis, became a partner. Moreover, all three have served as President of the Bellingham-Whatcom County Association of Realtors, and all three have been honored as Realtor of the Year by the local realtor association.

Follis Realtors Sales Division specializes in all types of residential and land listings and sales, consultations, market analysis, and property management. Their newly opened Commercial Division, created to help revitalize downtown Bellingham, specializes in commercial listings, sales, and leases in new offices adjacent to Follis Realtors' Prospect Center Mall location "across from the Museum." Additionally, Follis Realtors has the largest appraisal office north of the Seattle/Everett area, staffed by licensed appraisers.

For full-time, professional, friendly service – from a free consultation to a multi-million dollar transaction, Wm. T. Follis, Realtors remains here to serve all your real estate needs.

108 Prospect Street
Bellingham, WA 98225

Northwest Recycling

The Old Town area, including Northwest Recycling's current location, was once all tidelands. It was used in the 1950s as refuse fill areas for the population of Whatcom County.

In 1923, L.H. Parberry opened Parberry's Second Hand Store in what is now Old Town. In 1933, Lou Parberry Jr. started working in the store at the age of sixteen. Late in the same decade, father and son opened Parberry Scrap Yard. Parberry Jr. continued to run the business until the late 1980s.

Today, Northwest Recycling is still a family-owned operation committed to preserving the environment. They have established an environmental management program, and have taken the Whatcom Watershed Business Pledge to utilize recycled methods and products in their business operations. Northwest Recycling is also a member of ISRI (the Institute of Scrap Recycling Industries), Inc.

More committed than ever after 76 years in business, the Parberrys continue to work toward preserving our environment.

1999 Aerial photo from Dupont St. looking south.

Early 1900s – Picture taken from Whatcom Museum looking west

Brown's Beauty Supply

In the competitive world of wholesale and retail sales it's a rare business that can last 92 years. Of course, it's a rare business that can last 92 years in any form.

Nevertheless, in 1912 Brown's Beauty Supply sold barbering supplies to neighboring barbers from Dave Brown's horse and buggy. Today, they do the same, sans buggy, from their store in Bellingham.

Seeing a need for repair service in the industry, Brown brought John and Marino Gilson aboard as silent partners who could do mechanical and electrical work. The business continued to grow, and when Brown passed away in 1955, Marino Gilson continued the venture under the same name.

Burrell Hardan rose from part-time delivery boy to bookkeeper and, finally, to owner of Brown's Beauty Supply in 1968. Hardan retired in 1996, but his wife, Gloria, and his daughter, Kari Lynn, continue to head the business.

Brown's now operates seven stores, including locations in: Yakima, Wenatchee, Spokane, Mt. Vernon and, of course, stores on Meridian Street and Sunset Square in Bellingham.

BROWN'S
Beauty Supply

▲ *1915 – Brown's Beauty Supply. 211 E. Holly St.*

◀ *Kari Lynn Hardan in chair, 1957.*

Bellingham Lock & Safe

▲ *Bellingham Lock and Safe's location on Railroad Ave. (photo taken in the 1970's)*

The history of Bellingham Lock and Safe is synonymous with the history of Bellingham itself - both share recognizable names, landmarks, growth and 100 year anniversaries!

Bellingham Lock and Safe began in 1904 when Hugh Diehl and Pollard Nelson started a bicycle and locksmith business. Not long after that, Hugh left the business to pursue Indian brand motorcycles and eventually the Ford dealership. Pollard retained control of the business for many years but eventually sold the locksmith portion of the business to a gentleman named Bus Charles.

Bus ran the locksmith operation in a building in the 1300 block of Railroad Avenue until his death in the early 1950's. Four months later, Gus Newman moved to Bellingham to pick up the mantel. He was sole proprietor until present day owner Jim Vos joined him as partner in 1971. When Gus felt it was time to retire and move to Hawaii, his son-in-law Link Shadley took over his half of the business. Link and Jim expanded the business in the early 1980's until Jim took complete responsibility for Bellingham Lock and Safe when Link left to pursue other work. Because of the continuing growth, Jim moved the business to its current location on North State Street. The 10,000 square foot facility today houses a family of about 30 employees.

In the last few years, the company has evolved to offer a full complement of security products and services including fire suppression, contract hardware, surveillance systems, access controls and alarm systems. Because of this growth, the new name Security Solutions was introduced to more accurately reflect this complete offering.

Bellingham Lock and Safe will continue to provide superior lock and safe products and services, and through Security Solutions, address all security needs in Northwest Washington.

Bellingham Lock & Safe's current location on North State Street ▶

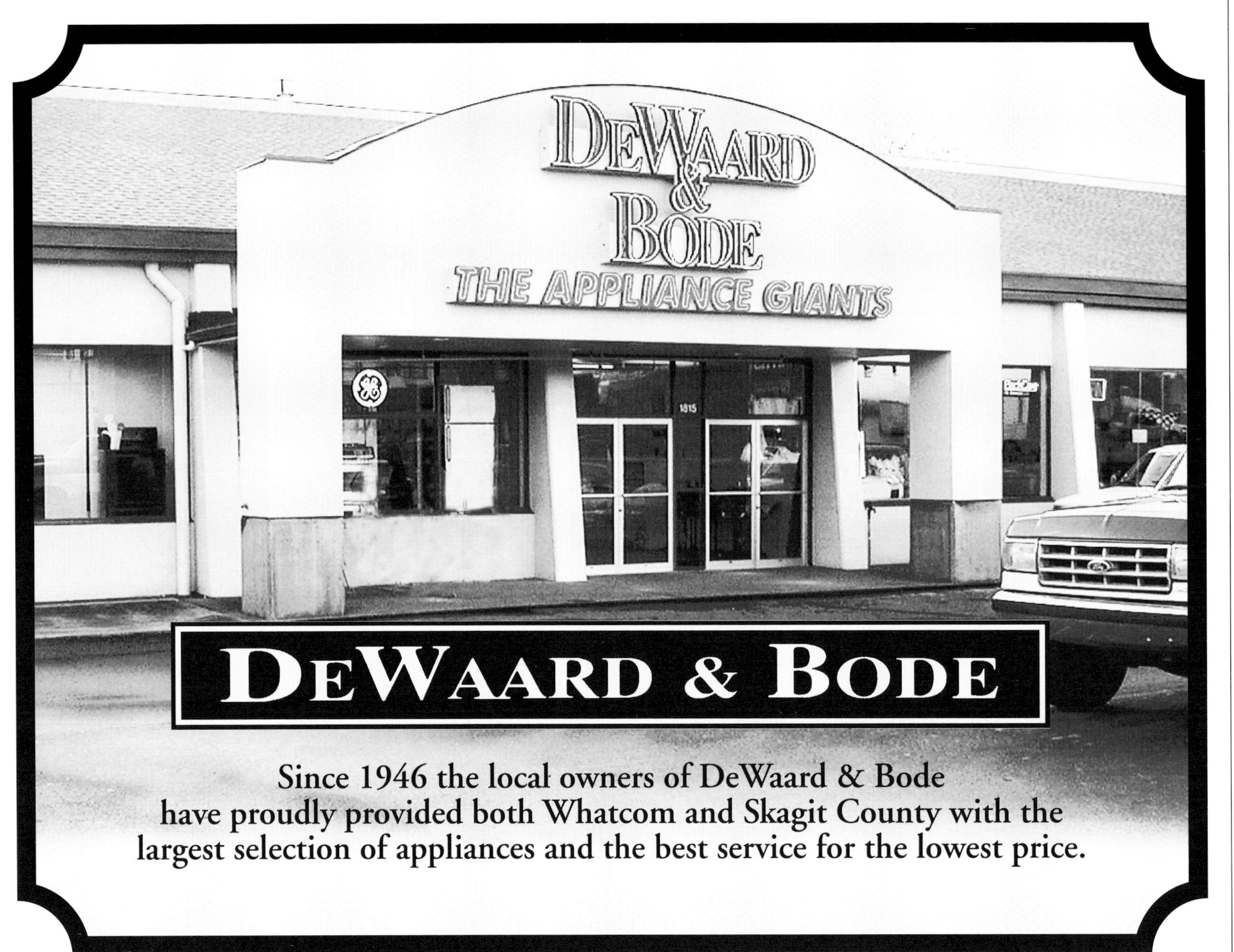
DeWaard & Bode
The Appliance Giants
1815
DeWaard & Bode
Since 1946 the local owners of DeWaard & Bode
have proudly provided both Whatcom and Skagit County with the
largest selection of appliances and the best service for the lowest price.

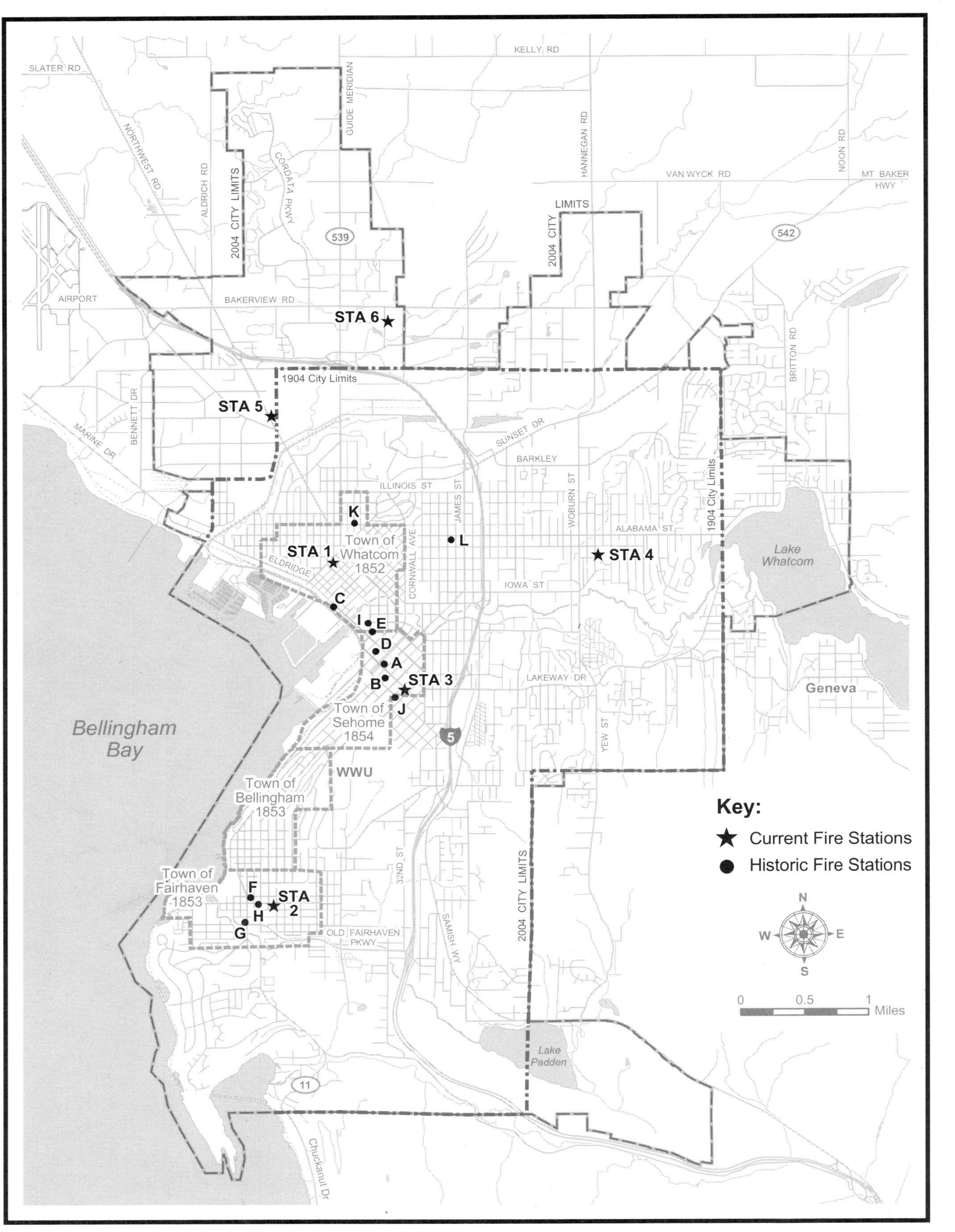
Key:
Current Fire Stations
Historic Fire Stations
N
W
E
S
0
0.5
1
Miles
STA 1
STA 2
STA 3
STA 4
STA 5
STA 6
A
B
C
D
E
F
G
H
I
J
K
L
Town of Whatcom 1852
Town of Sehome 1854
Town of Bellingham 1853
Town of Fairhaven 1853
WWU
Bellingham Bay
Lake Whatcom
Lake Padden
Geneva
1904 City Limits
2004 CITY LIMITS
KELLY RD
SLATER RD
GUIDE MERIDIAN
NORTHWEST RD
ALDRICH RD
CORDATA PKWY
HANNEGAN RD
NOON RD
VAN WYCK RD
MT BAKER HWY
539
542
AIRPORT
BAKERVIEW RD
BRITTON RD
BENNETT DR
MARINE DR
SUNSET DR
BARKLEY
ILLINOIS ST
JAMES ST
WOBURN ST
ALABAMA ST
CORNWALL AVE
ELDRIDGE
IOWA ST
LAKEWAY DR
YEW ST
5
32ND ST
SAMISH WY
OLD FAIRHAVEN PKWY
11
Chuckanut Dr